A SCARLET CORD OF HOPE

Sheryl Griffin speaks from personal experience and victory, offering hope and redemption for those in even the darkest storms.

When I read **A Scarlet Cord of Hope**, two things stood out: Sheryl has been through enough heartache for a dozen lifetimes and so is the perfect woman to write about very difficult issues like abuse, alcoholism, abortion and others. Sheryl truly offers hope to her readers, with practical tips and wise counsel, always pointing to God's generous gifts of forgiveness and redemption. Whatever troubles you're facing right now, **A Scarlet Cord of Hope** just might be the solid resource you need.

A beautiful story of hope from an equally beautiful lady with an incredible heart. In this book Sheryl removes her mask to reveal her story; her story will remind you there is *always* hope.

Sheryl Griffin clarifies the complicated for anyone struggling with issues of guilt and shame. After reading **A Scarlet Cord of Hope** you'll have new hope for living free of fear.

Sheryl's story paints a tangible picture of God's tender mercies for us all. Switch the names, genders or geography; the devastating events and emotional fallout will resonate with anyone who suffered loss. Lot's of us, growing up just like her, wondering if life is upside down or right side up, waiting for some responsible adult to come in and save the day. Thank God, for Sheryl's bravery to write it down for the rest of us. Bravo Sister!

Let her story lead you to believe, accept and know the freedom you can have in Christ!

Dana Russell Croce
Former Director, Piedmont Women's Center

Sheryl Griffin's writing is heartfelt, brutally honest and easy to read. You feel like you're sitting in her living room having a one-on-one conversation with her. I found myself relating my own life to hers and felt comforted that I wasn't alone. Her words will tug at your heart and you'll find yourself rooting for her through the trials and celebrating her triumphs!

This book is perfect to inspire the God-fearing person who's looking for love in all the wrong places, but also encourages those who've already found it. I found myself uplifted throughout this book. I appreciated Sheryl's willingness to be transparent in her quest to not only finding her own healing, but in helping others to find their own.

Victoria Koloff
Author, Non-Profit Executive, Christian Radio Show Host
Star on Lifetime Television's ***Preachers' Daughters***

A SCARLET
CORD OF HOPE

A SCARLET CORD OF HOPE

SHERYL GRIFFIN

WordCrafts

Published by WordCrafts Press
Tullahoma, TN 37388
www.wordcrafts.net

Acknowledgements

The Spirit of the Sovereign Lord is on me, because the Lord has anointed me to preach good news to the poor. He has sent me to bind up the brokenhearted, to proclaim freedom for the captives and release from darkness for the prisoners, to proclaim the year of the Lords favor and the day of vengeance of our God, to comfort all who mourn and provide for those who grieve in Zion to bestow on them a crown of beauty instead of ashes, the oil of gladness instead of mourning, and a garment of praise instead of a spirit of despair. They will be called oaks of righteousness, a planting of the Lord for the display of his splendor.

Isaiah 61:1-3

I am forever grateful to my husband Doug who has supported and encouraged me without hesitation. He continues to cheer me on with each and every thing I strive to do. He is without a doubt my KISA. Thank you for your unconditional love and support. I love you always!

My daughter Lauren - you will always be my angel girl. I am proud of who you are. I am grateful for our son-in-law Stephen - you are the answers to a mother's prayers. I love you both!

My son Garic - you are my sonshine forever and always. I know God has a plan and a purpose for your life and I look forward to watching it unfold in your life. I love you more!

I am thankful for a group of women who trusted me enough and were willing to take off their masks to help shape and mold the **Strands of Hope** questions at the end of each chapter. I am grateful for your input, encouragement and support. Kim Bindel, Annie Brown, René Claybrook, Kara Coats, Suzette Greer, Gwyn Griffeth, Karla Henry, Renee Patterson, Marcy Shore and Laura Spence - you will always be my Beauties.

I want to thank Mike and Paula Parker for your continued support and encouragement with this project. I am honored to be counted as one of your authors!

I also want to thank all of you who have taken time to email, write or speak to me over the years, encouraging me and letting me know I am not alone. Your words, tokens of love and appreciation, and prayers mean the world to me and I am grateful for *You*!

DEDICATION

This book is dedicated to all who walk through life with their scarlet cord of guilt, shame and fear. I pray that as you read this book you will begin to see your scarlet cord as a **Scarlet Cord of Hope**.

There is always *Hope*!

WHAT'S NEW

What is new?

If you're familiar with **A Scarlet Cord of Hope**, and have read the first edition, you will find this edition has more detail and information. I have also included a few pivotal chapters that have happened since the release of the original book in 2010. At the end of each chapter you'll still find the ***What I Know Now*** section that serves to give facts, insight or scriptures that correlate with that particular chapter. I have also added five ***Strands of Hope*** questions that were created to be self-reflective or used as a small group study. These questions are designed to help you in your journey towards hope.

CHAPTER 1

THE BEGINNING

For You formed my inward parts; You wove me in my mother's womb. I will give thanks to You, for I am fearfully and wonderfully made; Wonderful are Your works, and my soul knows it very well. My frame was not hidden from You, when I was made in secret, and skillfully wrought in the depths of the earth; Your eyes have seen my unformed substance. And in Your book were all written the days that were ordained for me, when as yet there was not one of them.

Psalm 139:13-16

The year was 1965 and life, as two young people knew it, was about to change. They exchanged wedding vows and promised to love and honor one another in front of the young man's family. Everyone knew why they were getting married, although it wasn't yet obvious.

I often wonder, if my mother had not become pregnant with me, would they have married? Would they have dated more than the few times they did before she became pregnant? Did they even love one another?

In spite of the odds against them, they did what was expected, and in turn each hoped for the best. Somewhere within the five and half years they were married the alcohol abuse, the accusations and the arguments opened the door for that hope to become a distant memory. The divorce that followed in 1972 was filled with anger and deceit.

As a mere child of five years old, I began my journey of

taking responsibility for other people's choices and behavior. I felt responsible for the demise of my family and the pain and anger that my parents openly showed in front of me. Each one telling stories of betrayal, abuse and instability.

I have memories of them arguing and yelling at one another. One time in particular they were in the kitchen and their voices quickly escalated. I was in the front room watching TV. As I glanced towards the kitchen a huge knot formed in my stomach. I couldn't see them, but I could hear the tone and the angry words. My dad realized I was listening and told me to go to my bedroom. I immediately jumped up and obeyed. As I sat on my bed, someone closed my bedroom door. I heard more yelling and then crying. I grabbed my doll and blanket, and I clutched them both tightly to my chest as tears began to form in my eyes.

I wanted to run to the kitchen and hug my parents in hopes of stopping them from the angry words they hurled at one another. I didn't understand why they were fighting; but I thought I was somehow responsible. *If only I had been better!* More guilt heaped upon my heart when I realized I didn't have the courage to open the door and tell them I was sorry.

I was in the middle of my kindergarten year when they agreed I would finish out the school year and continue to live with my dad, while my mom chose to move several hours away to live with her sister and brother-in-law. What happened after that depends on who you ask. According to my dad, my mom willingly signed legal documents giving him permanent custody of me before she moved out. My mom says she signed the documents, but there was a verbal agreement between them stating that at the end of the school year she would have permanent custody of me and I would live with her.

Shortly after my mom moved out, Dad and I left the duplex

where we had lived and moved in with his parents. My grandparents did everything they could to comfort and shield me from harsh reality of what was going on. I kept my feelings of guilt and sadness within my heart. I tried not to cry when I found myself sad or missing my mom, because I knew it made my dad feel bad.

After the initial divorce settlement, my dad gained permanent full custody of me. The judge awarded my mom with two yearly visitations - a week the day after Christmas and two weeks in the summer. She was allowed to call me once a week on Sunday evenings. My mom was shocked with the judge's order and vowed to keep fighting to gain full custody of me.

The court battles continued, and during one of the last hearings the judge wanted to hear from me. A Child Advocate Attorney was appointed to me.

I was prepped by both parents as to whom the woman I would be talking to was and the importance of what I was to say. The day finally arrived when I met with her. I was nervous. The situation weighed heavy on my heart. I tried to recall what both parents told me to say. I couldn't remember which parent told me what, and all of the earlier insecurities of my first years came rushing back, making me feel that no matter what I said, it was going to be the wrong answer. I wanted to believe that I held a magic key to getting my family back together. I wanted to say the right things to make it all work.

I don't recall all of her questions or how I answered, but I do recall telling her I wanted to live with both of my parents. Her response was short and filled with sympathy. "I am sorry Sheryl, that doesn't appear to be an option today." I left her office wondering if I said the right things to make everyone happy. I wondered if she would tell anyone what I said. I continued to keep everything locked inside.

What I Know Now

God purposed me to be born with the specific DNA of each of my parents. My parents may not have *planned* me, but God did. I was not an accident.

I was not responsible for the end of my parents' marriage.

It is natural for children of divorced parents to feel confused and want to live with both parents.

My parents (unintentionally) put me in the middle of their divorce and feelings for one another. This opened the door for guilt and shame to form in my mind and heart.

Divorce affects the whole family. Children and adults will cope differently. Children do not have the emotional maturity or verbal communication skills needed to fully communicate their feelings and they will often tell each parent what they think they want to hear.

Each year a million children are affected by divorce.

Strands of Hope

1. Read Psalm 139: 1-16. In what ways can you start choosing to live as if you believe this scripture is truth and meant for you?

2. Can you recall a time when you were a child and you wanted to please two adults with different agendas at the same time? What was the result?

3. Looking back with wisdom and insight that you have now, what would you tell a child who is struggling to please two adults who are in disagreement?

4. Has divorce or a fractured relationship affected your life (via yourself, parents, family, or friends)?

5. What are some key elements in helping a child cope
    in a situation with divorced parents?

Chapter 2

Visitation with My Mom

Peace I leave with you; My peace I give to you; not as the world gives do I give to you. Do not let your heart be troubled, nor let it be fearful.

John 14:27

Shortly after my parents' divorce was final, they each remarried on the same day, in same state, and each bride was 'with child'. I am the 'only child' between my parents. I am the oldest of six children in my dad's home and the oldest of two in my mom's home. Between the ages of six and fifteen, I grew up with my dad, stepmom, her two sons from a previous marriage, and three much younger half-siblings.

During our visits, my mom sometimes wanted to have *a talk* with me. These conversations always made me nervous. She told me terrible things about my dad, disturbing things about their marriage. Then she asked question, usually pertaining to herself. I frantically searched my memories, trying to find the *right* answer she was looking for. These questions usually pertained to things about her…"Sheryl, if you could change one thing about me, what would it be?" One time I recall nervously answering that I wished she would quit smoking. At the time it seemed like a safe answer. She took a longer-than-normal drag on her cigarette, smiled at my stepdad and said, "Well, that's not going to change." The smile she shared with my stepdad gave me relief. I had picked something that did not make her sad.

Time spent with my mom always included fun trips, new

6

clothes and quality time. My mom always made sure we went somewhere fun. There were trips to Disneyland, Knott's Berry Farm, parks and fairs. We enjoyed playing games together. One of my favorites, at that time, was The Peanut Butter and Jelly board game. I loved that game. I frequently cheated to ensure either my mom or I won, and that my stepdad lost. At my request, they also played *house* or *doctor* with me. When we played house, Mom and I were good people, while my stepdad was always relegated to being a stranger or a bad person. Whenever I got the doctor kit out, I was always the doctor and my mom the nurse, while my stepdad had to be the sick patient. It never failed: whatever ailed him, Dr. Sheryl had the cure - and it usually involved a shot, sometimes more than one shot. I made sure those injections went firmly into his arm. He was always a brave patient and had a smile on his face.

Looking back, I know that I was influenced by my dad's comments about my stepdad. Unfortunately, I was not very kind to him. It's not that I was a competitive person. I didn't have to win the games, as long as *he* didn't win. He seemed to understand that the reason I responded to him the way I did was because of my situation.

All too soon each visit reached another ending. As we headed towards the airport, I knew that our relationship would be back to a short phone call on the weekends and the homemade cards she would send me in the mail. It would be six months before we would see each other again.

On the way home to my dad's house, I would play back the picture of my mom in my mind - her beautiful, long blonde hair, her makeup applied to perfection, even her smell. She frequently applied Rose Milk hand lotion, so she always smelled of roses. Her home was always nice and clean, and had a loving feel - beds always made, laundry always put away, ashtrays always emptied and cleaned at night, and cupboards were orderly, dishes never stayed in the sink, counters always clean and free of clutter. The coffee tables and shelves were always free of dust and the floors were always vacuumed, mopped and swept. During meal times we sat at the dinner table as a family. We talked, laughed and played together.

Our visits together were always fun - that is with the exception of the last few days. Those were spent with little communication and an underlining sadness. The reality of not seeing each other for months on end was hard. During one particular visit, as our time was ending, my mom and stepdad asked if I wanted to live with them. Of course, I said yes! The rest of the day our conversations revolved around the possibility of moving, changing my name…and me never seeing my dad and his family again.

I cried when I began to understand all of the implications. I wanted to live with my mom; but I also wanted to still live with my dad. I was told to call my dad and tell him that I was not coming home. I cried as I told him I was not coming home. I lied and told him it was my idea and I wanted this.

At the time, it seemed only minutes before my dad was at the front door with a Sheriff. The reality is, it must have taken hours, possibly even days, since he had to make a plane reservation, contact his attorney and meet with the local Sheriff's department. As my dad and the Sheriff stood at the door, my mom calmly gathered my things and put them in the suitcase. She hugged me and with tears in her eyes told me to never forget how much she loved me.

My dad and I rode to the airport in the back of the Sheriff's car. As we settled in the back seat, we both cried and hugged. I felt responsible for the pain and anguish that I saw in my dad, but I also felt responsible for the tears and heartache I saw in my mom as I left. I cried the entire flight home. As far as I know, no legal action was taken against my mom.

I felt guilt for wanting to live with my mom and for saying 'yes' to their plan, even though once I realized what it meant, I didn't want it. I felt guilt for telling my dad I did not want to come home. I felt fear and guilt when I saw the Sheriff at the door. In my child's mind, the police only come to get the "bad guys."

I didn't know how to communicate what was going on inside my mind and heart. No one said a word about it afterwards, not my dad, my mom or my grandparents. It was pushed under the rug, never to be brought up again. Sweeping things under the rug and not talking about them anymore would continue as a life-long pattern that would ultimately lead to my first panic attack.

What I Know Now

Parents should reserve their opinions and negative stories of one another to other adults, not to the children. This can have a damaging affect on the children.

Never allow yourself to sweep things under the rug, no matter how difficult the situation is. Age appropriate communication is vital. Not talking about a situation doesn't make it go away.

Children should not be the confidant of their parents' secrets or feelings. The child is unable to process such things on an adult level. This creates a huge burden for the child and sets them up for shame and guilt.

In divorce situations it is important to focus on what is best for the child(ren) involved and not necessarily what the adults want.

Strands of Hope

    1. Reflect on a time from childhood when you were

affected by the feeling of guilt. Did you sweep it under the rug or have you been able to move forward with it?

2. If you had an opportunity to talk with a friend who is struggling through brokenness, what advice would you encourage him/her with?

3. Is it ever okay to disregard a court order or judges ruling? When? Why?

4. Do you struggle with presenting a good image on the outside and yet you're a "mess" on the inside? What can you do to begin the process of taking off your mask and allowing yourself to be real with those around you? Read 2 Timothy 1:7.

5. Have the actions of another person caused you to carry unnecessary guilt? What can you do now remove this burden of guilt from your life?

CHAPTER 3

Family Life at My Dad's

The Lord is near to the brokenhearted, and saves those who are crushed in spirit.

Psalm 34:18-19

As soon as my dad and stepmom married, my dad wanted an instant family. He felt things would fall into place more naturally if I started calling my stepmom, *Mom.* I did *not* want to do this. I felt uncomfortable. They hadn't dated long and I felt as if I didn't know her. I saw her as a threat, because I was hopeful that someday my parents would reconcile. Even though they both had made it clear this would never happen; I still had hope. I also worried that if I started calling her *Mom,* it would hurt my real Mom's feelings.

But my dad was determined. He took me on car rides, just me and him, and he used the time to try to convince me. He told me how important it was to him that I do this (guilt). He told me how happy it would make her (taking responsibility for someone else's feelings over mine). He never asked me if I wanted to do this or how I felt about it. He simply told me what he wanted and he expected me to follow through.

I finally said it - "Mom." That one little word seemed to make everyone happy; everyone but me. Saying and doing things to make others happy, at my own expense, would develop into a pattern of behavior that would prime me for an abusive relationship. I was careful not to reference her as "Mom" when I was talking to my real Mom though.

I was close to my three youngest siblings. I willingly took on the role of big sister and caregiver. As much as I wanted to be the only child, I also loved being needed and wanted by my siblings. As siblings, we got along and were protective of one another. It was rare when one of the youngest was not in bed with me at night. This innocent family routine would later come back to haunt me in my first marriage.

As a family, we always struggled financially, between my Dad getting laid off from his job, workers' union strikes, a serious foot injury and raising six children, money was always an issue. This was difficult to accept. No child wants to be 'less than' when compared with her peers. We were told to tell the cashier at the local store, "Please hold this check for a week." Fortunately, they knew our family situation, so they were always agreeable. I was aware that my friends never had to say this when they went to the store, so I'd walk around the store until I was sure no one I knew was at the checkout.

With the exception of the new clothes that my mom bought during our visits, I always wore hand-me-downs. Our home and vehicles always looked unsightly and impoverished. Our family often qualified for welfare, food stamps and free lunches at school. My stepmom sometimes babysat just to bring in a little extra cash. With two adults, six kids and the "extras" my stepmom kept, the house was always chaotic and unkempt. No one really cared about outward appearances there. We all just did what we had to do to get to the next day.

There was nothing significant about our home life outside of our finances. Our home just...*was*. We lived in a middle class neighborhood in a three bedroom, one bathroom home. The house had blue carpet and black and white curtains with red sheers. It was furnished with a few items my step mom brought with her to the marriage, and a few pieces my dad brought along from his. My dad's parents gave the rest to us.

As children, we had many chores to do. It seemed our dryer was always broken, so it was my job to hang the laundry outside on the clothesline. With eight people in the family, there was always lots of laundry to do. If I left clothes on the line too long, pincher bugs would invade the clean laundry. I hated those bugs, and I hated the way the laundry always felt stiff and scratchy from the sun and wind drying them out.

While dusting, vacuuming and emptying ashtrays was never a priority in our home, washing the dirty dishes was. My two stepbrothers and I had to take turns washing dishes every night, but the kitchen was still never really clean. Since we never really washed the dishes very well in the first place, it always seemed that I had to wash a "clean" cup if I wanted something to drink. We were not required to make our beds as long as things were picked up off the floor at night. It didn't matter if we just shoved things under the beds or in the closets.

Having one bathroom with eight people only added to the stress. The door didn't have a lock, so unless you pulled the drawer from the bathroom counter out, as a way to block the door from opening, privacy was never guaranteed. The rough towels, made all the more scratchy from drying outside in the sun, made bath time less than a pleasurable experience, and the pungent smell of old urine was a constant.

Dinner times at our home were always quick and quiet. The kids sat at the kitchen table, while my dad and stepmom ate in the front room. This made it easy when we had things on our dinner plate that we did not like. We simply tossed the food under the table where the dog could clean it up or we swept it outside after dinner.

Even though there was nothing abusive our home I yearned

for the return of my *ideal* family - my life before my parents' divorce. I couldn't let go of my child-like fantasy of pretending that my parents might someday love one another again. I also deeply craved an emotional relationship with my dad. I knew that something was missing. The only time we ever connected was when he and I would visit his parents. Away from the distractions of our home life, my dad would talk to me and connect with me. I looked forward to those visits when he would bring out his high school year books and tell me stories of his high school sweetheart or his friends.

There were other things he talked to me about during those times. He told me that my mother left us; that she had *problems*. He told me she left us just like she did her first husband. She had married her first husband at age fifteen and gave birth to a son. His name was LeRoy. My dad told me she chose to walk away from her son and her husband.

I never asked questions or made any comments during those conversations, because in my heart I knew he was probably making this up. My mom had never mentioned I had a brother before, and no one else had ever said anything to me about him.

During one summer visit when I was ten years old, towards the end of our visit my mom and stepdad sat me down, explaining they had some news to share with me. I wondered what it could be. They proceeded to tell me that before my mom married my dad she had been married to another man and that she had a baby - a boy named LeRoy. I sat there shocked and unsure of what to say or how to respond. I didnt want them to know my dad had told about this years before and I didn't want to believe him. I felt tremendous guilt for thinking my dad had made that up.

I met LeRoy for the first time summer of 1977. It appeared

to be a good thing and most of the time when I was visiting my mom they also made a point to have him there as well. Then on one particular visit he wasn't there. I asked if he was coming and my mom's response was, "No, he won't be coming to visit any more." I cried. I didn't understanding why, but knew it was better not to ask questions.

As time passed I continued weaving new strands into my rapidly expanding scarlet cord of guilt. It started with me taking on the initial guilt of my parents' unhappiness and divorce. Even childhood privileges had the potential to increase my feelings of guilt. I had visitation with my mom twice each year, and talked with her on the phone every week. My stepbrothers didn't have that privilege because their natural father didn't make the effort to keep in contact. It wasn't my fault, but I felt guilty just the same. While my dad's parents and my aunt were kind and loving to all my stepsiblings, they were devoted to me and often invited me to spend weekends at their homes - invitations they did not extend to my stepsiblings. Once again, guilt over something I had no control over weighed heavy on my heart.

I knew it hurt my stepmom, and I thought she resented me because of it. To her credit, she never treated me any differently. Looking back, I know it was my own feelings that I was projecting onto her.

What I Know Now

Parents should not coerce or *guilt* their child(ren) into feeling something that they do not feel. As the adult you need to make the right decision for your child, but it's important that you hear your child's heart and consider all costs before you enforce something that is important to you.

Open communication is important in any relationship but much more so with blended families. These families are not only dealing with the realities of divorce, but also the

15

concepts of blending two different families into one.

Years after my mother telling me my brother LeRoy would no longer be visiting I gained a greater understanding of the situation. LeRoy had apparently brought drugs into their home, and instead of helping him or setting boundaries they chose to cut all ties. Their goal was specifically to protect my younger sister and me.

Shame gives you a feeling that says I am bad. Guilt gives you the feeling you did something bad. Both of these feelings can be healthy and needed, but it is important to maintain a good balance, which I did not.

Strands of Hope

1. Is there a time when you were coerced into a decision that you felt obligated to follow through on? Read Psalm 34:18 and Zephaniah 3:17

2. What are the challenges and blessings of a blended family?

3. If you're struggling with guilt and shame, you need to find the root of the problem and deal with it. It's important to forgive yourself (and others). Romans 8:1 tell us "There is no condemnation for those who are in Christ." If you have accepted Christ in your heart, there is no longer any reason to allow guilt and shame to control you. Read Ephesians 1:7 and Colossians 1:13-14. Encourage and affirm someone this week with one of these scriptures (a note in the mail, a treat with scripture attached, pray one of the scriptures over them, etc)

4. Facing issues and moving forward in a healthy manner requires *heart* work. To realize why you made a choice, allowed a behavior or respond the way you do to certain things, you must get to the root of the matter. Is there an area you are willing to face and

move forward in?

5. Author, Liz Curtis Higgs has said, "You can't out sin God's mercy." Do you believe this? Why or why not? Find a scripture to confirm your belief.

CHAPTER 4

CHAPTER 4

TEENAGE HORMONES

God, being rich in mercy, because of His great love with which He loved us, even when we were dead in our transgressions, made us alive together with Christ (by grace you have been saved.)

Ephesians 2:4-5

When I was twelve years old my mom and stepdad moved closer to where I was living with my dad. They were now only a short, thirty-minute drive away. To my great surprise and joy, my dad agreed to allow me to spend more time with my mom. In addition to our regular summer and Christmas visits, I got to spend whole weekends with her once every month.

The summer before my freshman year of high school, I began to blossom into a young woman. I had always struggled with issues of self-image. I never felt pretty. I had no self-confidence. I certainly wasn't trendy or one of the popular girls, yet that summer I started getting a lot of attention from boys. I was confused.

I thought the attention I was getting would eventually equal love, and I fell into the *secret* pattern. I was willing to have *secret* relationships with a football player or a popular guy in class, even though these boys usually had a *non-secret* relationship with a cheerleader or a popular girlfriend. My heart always hoped that someone would open their eyes and say, "Sheryl, I love *you!* You're the one I want and need."

That never happened. I don't excuse what those high school

boys did, but I don't blame them either. I was an easy target. I was willing, because I was hopeful.

There is a quote from one of my favorite movies, *That Thing You Do*, that I just love. The main girl character has just opened her eyes and heart to the awful truth of her boyfriend's true character, and how he has treated her. She is brave enough to see it, acknowledge it and move away from it. She tells him, "I wasted too many kisses on you." I too was wasting too many kisses on undeserving young men.

My first serious relationship was with Richard, a boy in my graduating class. We started dating in October, 1980. It was our freshman year. He seemed to fill my need for attention and love, but he had a reputation as a partier, and I had to compete with drugs and alcohol for his attention. While I never drank or did drugs, I allowed myself to protect him and cover for him when he did.

During the middle of my sophomore year of high school, after a confrontation with my dad, I asked if I could go to my mom's house for an extra weekend. Dad said, "No." I didn't understand his reluctance to let me go, so I mustered up the courage to ask, "Why?" My questioning only made him mad.

"Fine," he said. "You want to go live with your mom, then go ahead."

Before I realized what I was saying I replied, "Okay, I want to live with my mom."

My dad was so devastated that he refused to talk to me. He called my grandfather to come over to talk to me instead. I will never forget the tears in my grandfather's eyes as he asked me, "Why?"

Through my own tear-filled eyes, I whispered, "I don't know. I just want to."

I didn't know how to tell him that I had wanted out for a long time. I was tired of the endless responsibilities of babysitting and chores. I saw life at my mom's as an escape. I knew she wanted me to live with her, and I thought that if I lived with her, she would no longer be sad. It would be as if I were coming *home* to her.

My dad refused to talk to me for over a year. Even though I was excited about living with my mom, I felt reprehensible in my dad's eyes. The guilt that came with my decision only added weight to the scarlet cord that was inexorably wrapping itself like an invisible noose around my neck.

From age 15 to 18, I lived with my mom, stepdad and younger sister. Life at my mom's was vastly different from the home life at my dad's. Having only one sibling in the home made huge difference. I didn't have the responsibilities that I had at my dad's house. Things were always quite and the house was always clean. Money was no longer an issue - no hand-me-downs, no free lunch line, no food stamps. Things were clean, orderly and looked good...at least from the outside looking in. Appearances mattered here.

What I Know Now

I was looking for an emotional connection, and I was willing to sacrifice my needs or desires if I thought someone loved me.

I had an unhealthy view of relationships and boundaries. I was a primed enabler and co-dependent.

One of the reasons I felt that my first serious relationship seemed to fill all of my voids was because it fit the patterns I was use to. His drug and alcohol use kept us from getting too close and I subconsciously thought that I could help him.

My dad took my decision to live with my mom personally.

He felt I was choosing my mom over him.

Strands of Hope

1. Looking back at your 15 year-old self, what advice or wisdom would you give yourself?

2. Allowing secret relationships and wasting too many kisses on undeserving young men was a sign of not respecting myself. What is something you may be doing that could be a sign of not respecting yourself?

3. When we look to others to fulfill our needs and desires, it opens the door for the enemy to chip away at our confidence, dignity and self-respect. We ignore the red flags and listen to the lies. Read Matthew 16:23, John 8:44, Matthew 4:3, and John 10:10. What do these scriptures tell us about the enemy?

4. Here are four common traits that someone who struggles with being co-dependent may have:
   - Find needy people to take care of.
   - Have an over developed sense of responsibility.
   - Have difficulty saying "No" and or setting boundaries.
   - Self blame and constantly put self down.

5. Do you see yourself in any of the above co-dependent character traits? If so, which trait seems to have the biggest influence in your life? Write down at least three goals, scriptures or choices that will move you towards freedom in that area.

CHAPTER 5

LIVING WITH MY MOM

*If we confess our sins He is faithful and just to forgive
us our sins and to cleanse us from all unrighteousness.*

1 John 1:9

I was 15 years old when I chose to live with my mom and
stepdad. This involved a lot of change: new school, new
neighborhood, new expectations and new rules at home.
While I kept in touch with my old friends and boyfriend, the
30-minute drive put a huge distance between us.

As soon as I was settled in at my mom's house, knowing I
had a boyfriend, she asked me if I was sexually active. I was
embarrassed and didn't feel comfortable talking about that
subject. At a very early age, my mom began giving me *the sex
talks* and even offered to show me pictures of naked men.
Embarrassed, I declined. I know she wanted me to be open
and honest with her, but every time she talked about sex it
only made me feel uncomfortable. She didn't approach it
from a parental or even educational point of view. It was
more like trying to be two girlfriends talking about it. The
problem was; this was my mom, not my friend. I denied
being sexually active, and settled into a routine of listening to
her stories and thoughts on sex without sharing any of my
own thoughts.

Because I never said anything during these conversations,
she became suspicious.

"Do you think you might be pregnant?" she asked.

"No," I answered.

Richard and I had dated for a year before I moved in with my mom, and we started having sex within a few months. I was foolish and naïve enough to think I could have sex and not get pregnant. I know my mom wanted me to be as open with her as she was with me, but I couldn't bring myself to open up. I felt guilty.

With all of the talk of sex and pregnancy, I began to think I probably needed to start using some form of birth control. A friend and I decided we'd skip out of school early one day and go to a facility where young girls could get free birth control and condoms. We each forged a note saying we had a dental appointment and needed to leave at noon. Unbeknownst to either of us the school always called the parents to alert them that the student is on their way home for their appointment.

We went to the facility where we were both examined, given birth control pills and condoms and instructed to come back for a follow-up visit in a few weeks. We made it home before either of our parents suspected anything - or so we thought. As soon as I got home, I put the birth control pills and condoms inside a hidden drawer in my jewelry box.

That night I could sense there was something going on, but neither my mom nor stepdad said a word to me. Although it seemed eerily quiet to me, I felt confident that I had gotten away with it. I was relieved that I wouldn't have to expose myself to my mom and that I would now be protected from any potential pregnancy.

The next day everyone woke up and prepared for the day as usual. My Mom and my stepdad took my sister to daycare, then went on to work. I went to school and didn't think twice about anything. What I didn't know was that after they dropped off my sister, they came back to the house and went through everything in my room. Apparently, although the school had called them right after I left for my *dental appointment*, they waited until the next day to go through my things. They wanted to find evidence before they confronted me. They assumed I was doing drugs.

After searching through my closet, under my bed, in my drawers and everywhere else that might have been a hiding place, they came upon my jewelry box.

The jewelry box had a small lock on the front, and a tiny key to unlock it. I always kept the key inside the jewelry box because I never locked it. I hadn't locked it this time either, yet it was locked. In my haste to secure my stash, I must have done something to trip the latch. They broke the lock and lifted the flap on the bottom that was my *secret* compartment. Inside they saw the birth control pills and the condoms.

As I walked home from school, I realized something was going on. Mom and my stepdad were home, which was unusual for that time of day. I anxiously considered my options. If they did know I had forged a note, I was unsure what my punishment might be. I figured I would be told to pack my things and be sent back to my dad's house. I decided the best thing was just to walk in and hope for the best.

"Sit down," my mom ordered as soon as I entered. She then proceeded to tell me she knew all about how I had forged a note and cut school. She demanded to know where I went and whom I was with. I sat there crying for what seemed like hours, afraid to tell her the truth. It was only when she began accusing me of doing drugs that I told her where my friend and I had gone. She was furious and hurt that I had lied to her.

"I asked if you were having sex, and you said 'No,'" she accused.

The truth is, I didn't want her to know the truth about me. I felt ashamed. The majority of my close friends were not sexually active, and those who were had a wild reputation. I didn't want that reputation. I didn't want anyone to think badly of me.

Even though my mom did her best to talk to me at an early age about sex, it felt wrong to me. I was uncomfortable talking so openly about the subject with her. I feared that if she knew the truth, she might not love me anymore, that she might regret letting me move in with her.

Once the truth came pouring out, my mom insisted that I have a gynecological exam with her doctor, which included a pregnancy test. A few days later, we received a call from the doctor's office. The nurse asked to speak to me.

"Sheryl," the nurse said, "your pregnancy test is positive".

I felt an odd combination of shame and sadness. I cried. I didn't want to get off the phone and tell my mom and stepdad the news.

"There is no other option," my mom said as soon as I told her the results of my pregnancy test. "You have to get an abortion."

I wanted to keep my baby, even though I had no idea what being a parent really meant. My mom made it clear they would not help me support or raise a baby; if I kept the baby, I would have to go back to my dad's house. She made sure I understood how mad and disappointed my dad would be. She believed my dad would never support me with a baby.

It's possible that my boyfriend's parents may have supported me, but their oldest son's girlfriend was also pregnant. I think everyone was relieved that I agreed to go through with an abortion. I didn't feel like I had any other choice.

I was put under anesthesia for the procedure. I cried as they put the mask over my face. I wanted to scream "No!" but after a few quick breathes I fell into a deep, drugged sleep. I awakened with a nurse standing next to me, telling everything went smoothly and that I would be fine.

We returned home and things went back to normal. My mom and stepdad remained suspicious that I was using drugs, and they made it clear that while they believed in sexual freedom they were not going to allow it in their home. The rug was pulled over the subject and no one talked about the pregnancy or abortion.

At the time I didn't know much about abortion. My mom and stepdad told me even though I was pregnant, it wasn't a real baby yet, just a mass of cells. They assured me this was the best decision. I didn't believe them. I didn't agree with them. But I did what was expected of me. I didn't feel I had a choice.

This situation added to the weight of my scarlet cord. I was ashamed that I lied to my mom, and more than anything else I felt a deep guilt for the abortion. My boyfriend and I continued in our relationship, but in an off-and-on-again dependency. Now that we no longer lived in the same city, the time we spent together was limited. When we were "off," I slipped easily back into the pattern of seeking out unhealthy, sometimes secretive, relationships. I wanted to be someone else, but I didn't know how. The weight of my guilt and shame was beginning to smother me.

What I Know Now

A 1996 statistic said that 1.37 million abortions are performed every year, and 43% of all women will have an abortion by the age of 45.

The affects from abortion are life long. Unfortunately, forgiveness does not come with an eraser.

There are other options besides abortion. Today there are many resources available to help you if you decide to keep your baby or want to consider adoption.

I know my baby is in Heaven. An aborted baby is not any different from a baby that has been miscarried or stillborn; I believe they go straight into the arms of Jesus. I know now that I am forgiven and I accept that, but I will always regret having an abortion.

Strands of Hope

1. Sex is often an uncomfortable subject to talk about, but it's important that we understand sex from God's perspective. What do you consider the consequences that sex outside of marriage to be? What does purity bring into a relationship?

2. Have you ever struggled with forgiving yourself? Have you felt you may have crossed the line of no return? Read Psalm 103:12, Isaiah 44:22 and Ephesians 1:7.

3. Choose one of the scriptures above, write it on an index card and put it in a place where you will see it daily as a reminder of God's love, mercy and forgiveness.

4. Sweeping things under the rug and not confronting them is a behavior pattern that hinders you from moving forward. Is there an area in your life that you repeatedly place under the rug? What are you willing to do to change this pattern?

5. The impact of abortion can hinder the spiritual growth of a person for years. Many men and women are walking in chains of guilt and shame due to their choice or involvement in abortion. Forgiving ourselves and accepting God's forgiveness is not the same as condoning our sin (whether it's abortion or

any other past or present sin). Is there an area of sin that you have not confessed and repented of that is hindering your spiritual growth? Read Psalm 32:5 and 1 John 1:9.

CHAPTER 6

ACCEPTING CHRIST

*That if you confess with your mouth that Jesus as Lord,
and believe in your heart that God raised Him from the
dead, you will be saved.*

Romans 10:9

L ess than a year into living with my mom and stepdad,
they decided to move to another city about thirty
minutes away. This meant living farther from my
boyfriend, starting another new school and making new
friends. They wanted to live in an area that was closer to
their work and my younger sister's day care, which was
located in a church. My younger sister wanted to attend
services there, and I decided to join her. Every Sunday the
pastor drove the church bus into different neighborhoods to
pick up children for Sunday school. My mom and stepdad
weren't interested in going, but they had no objection to us
attending. While I believed there was a God, I didn't know
much about the Bible.

As a young child growing up in my dad's home, there was a
short season when my younger siblings and I attended a local
church. They had a bus that drove into all of the
neighborhoods filling the bus with as many children as
wanted to go. I enjoyed going, but I felt out of place. I
wasn't familiar with the Bible stories, but I was intrigued. I
wanted to understand, but I was not bold enough to ask
questions. It seemed as if all the other children already knew
these stories and Bible verses. I felt embarrassed and found

myself sitting quietly, trying not to attract any attention. I was afraid of being called on.

With this lingering memory of church, I longed to understand the Bible. The church had a small youth group. I enjoyed going and made friends quickly. For the first time in my life, I felt like I was beginning to understand the Gospel. I accepted Jesus as my savior and decided to get baptized. All the while my scarlet cord remained firmly wrapped around my neck as a reminder of all of the things I did or did not do. It felt like there were two sides to me. One side wanted all that Jesus offered - grace, mercy and forgiveness; and the other side that held all of my condemnation, insecurities and low self-esteem. I couldn't connect the two sides. I struggled with allowing Jesus to accept me for who I was and who I wanted to be.

I developed two core groups of friends; my church friends and my non-church friends. My non-church friends had no idea that I had accepted Christ as my savior or had been baptized. My church friends were completely in the dark about the different life I led when I was away from them. Although it was mentally exhausting keeping up with two different sides of myself, it was comfortable in an odd sort of way. I was able to be who I wanted to be, and who I thought I deserved to be, all at the same time.

At church, I really enjoyed being around the youth pastor and his wife. I saw something in their life, something between them, that I had not seen before. I couldn't pin point what it was, but I was drawn to it. There seemed to be a genuine joy within their hearts. They showed tender love and care towards one another. They lived what they preached. They had a heart to serve and to share the Gospel with anyone who would listen.

I loved hearing them share about how they met and how the

youth pastor pursued his wife. When he asked her to go on a date with him, she told him she would go out with him, but he had to understand there was another man in her life, a man who meant more to her than anyone else in the world. At first, he didn't understand, but then she told him, "His name is Jesus." From that moment on he wanted to know more about this Jesus. He wanted to know who this man was, that a young woman would make Him a priority in her life. He wanted the peace and joy that filled her heart. They dated with boundaries and agreed to stay pure until marriage. They knew they wanted to pursue ministry and share their story and hope with young people.

While I loved their story, hearing it made me sad. I realized I would never be able to have that. I had already crossed the line of purity, became pregnant and had an abortion. Although I didn't feel I deserved the hope they shared, I longed for the unconditional love they had with one another.

I went to church every Sunday morning and Wednesday night. The youth group went on a few excursions and weekend retreats. I saw Amy Grant at a local amusement park and was overwhelmed at how many *perfect* people I saw at her concert. I was sure no one there had ever walked in the shoes that I was walking in. I desired to change the patterns I was in, but I lacked the tools and the foundation to change these behaviors.

My boyfriend and I started drifting further apart as the long distance began to wear on our relationship. During my junior year in high school, after being together for almost two and half years, we broke up for the last time. I was sad, but I was tired of having a long-distance relationship. Plus, my mom and stepdad made it clear that they didn't really like him, which made seeing each other even more difficult.

I had two friends, sisters, who went to my high school and

31

my church. They had an older brother who had already graduated. We started dating and before I knew it the relationship turned sexual. We hid that aspect of our relationship from everyone; we were living a lie. We continued to attend church, but also continued opening doors that God ordained only for a husband and wife. This relationship lasted less than a year, but all of the guilt and shame from it just added to the weight of my scarlet cord, contributing to my feelings of shame and worthlessness.

I wanted to be strong, but I felt so weak. I wanted unconditional love and acceptance. I yearned for a clean slate and forgiveness. It was hard to imagine that Jesus loved me as much as the Bible said. I certainly didn't forgive myself, so how could God forgive me? By not confronting these issues I marched forward into unhealthy patterns and behaviors.

What I Know Now

I was looking for an emotional connection and was willing to sacrifice my needs or desires if I thought someone loved me.

I had an unhealthy view of relationships and boundaries.

The enemy is like a roaring lion seeking someone to devour (in whatever way he can) 1 Peter 5:8.

There is no such thing as a *perfect* Christian. Jesus isn't looking for you to get all cleaned up and to figure things out before you come to Him. He wants you just as you are.

Strands of Hope

1. What do you consider healthy boundaries in the following relationships; dating, friendship, marriage, family and employee/employer?

2. Being emotionally connected to someone requires that you both share on a deep level, trusting one another and allowing yourself to be vulnerable. Do

you feel emotionally connected to Christ? Read Psalm 55:17, Isaiah 43:2 and Hebrews 4:12-13.

3. Is there something in your life that is hindering you from allowing others to get close to you? Read Galatians 5:1

4. Take the opportunity this week to encourage someone in their walk with God with scripture, a poem or an encouraging word.

5. Believing we have to be perfect and all cleaned up before we come to the throne of grace is a lie from the enemy. What are other lies that hinder us from experiencing a quality relationship with God?

CHAPTER 7

AND THEN CAME MARRIAGE

Love is patient, love is kind and is not jealous; love does not brag and is not arrogant, does not act unbecomingly; it does not seek its own, is not provoked, does not take into account a wrong suffered, does not rejoice in unrighteousness, but rejoices with the truth; bears all things, believes all things, hopes all things, endures all things.

1 Corinthians 13:4-7

The beginning of my senior year of high school I was not as active in church or as involved with my "church friends." That's when I got involved with a guy I knew from school. He was well known all over campus as a party guy who hung out with all the popular kids. He also had a reputation for having a temper. Although he graduated the year before, I often saw him on campus. One evening he came into the store where I worked. While I helped him locate an item, we started talking. One thing led to another and he came back after I got off work. I was flattered. He pursued and I followed.

I thought I could love him, care for him and help him. We started dating exclusively from the very beginning. He was charming and attentive. He always wanted to be around me and to know what I was doing. I felt special because he wanted to spend so much time with me. We had only been dating a few short months when, on Christmas Day in 1983, he asked me to marry him.

My mom and stepdad acted as if they were happy for us and

34

had no reservations whatsoever at the thought of us becoming engaged at such a young age - I was seventeen and he was eighteen. There was a part of me that wanted my mom and stepdad to question us, to step in and make us wait. But there were no questions; only congratulations and talk of when we thought we wanted to get married.

My mom and stepdad had a plan should anyone in the family get in trouble or need immediate help. They created a code word we could use to let other family members know, "I need you. There is something wrong." The word could easily fit into an everyday kind of sentence. I don't know how long they had this word or how it came about. To my knowledge, I am the only one in the family who has ever used it.

We hadn't been engaged for very long before I needed to use that code word. While on a break between classes I went to see my fiancé at the room he was renting. No one else was home. He had been drunk since the night before, and continued to drink while I was there. Even though I had a lot of exposure to drunkenness within my family, I had never experienced the fear that I felt that day. In the midst of his rants he showed me a gun and said he knew how to kill people, including me, if he wanted. To say I was frightened is an understatement. He wouldn't let me go back to school. He wanted me to stay there with him.

I had no idea if I was going to die that day or not. I felt like a prisoner. At one point the UPS man came to the door to deliver a package. I wanted to slip him a note, but I couldn't figure out a way to do it without getting caught.

My fiancé seemed to vacillate between anger and tears. He raged at everything and nothing in particular. He got so angry with me that he pulled my engagement ring off, told me I didn't deserve it and then proceeded to swallow it!

I prayed for God to protect me and to get me out of there

alive. I felt frozen in time. As scared as I was, I also felt sad for him. It was obvious he was dealing with a multitude of issues, although I had no idea what exactly they were. I felt powerless to help him. I tried to comfort him and to assure him of my love. I wanted to show him that I *did* deserve his love and his ring. He started crying and said he knew I must not love him anymore.

It was surreal. I felt like I was in a dream. I had never been around anyone who acted like this. I felt an odd combination of compassion and fear all muddled together. I believed he was capable of doing all the violent things he said, yet I loved him and wanted to help him.

He stopped drinking and even appeared to be sobering up a little. I knew this was a good chance to make my escape, but I also knew I needed a good reason for him to agree to let me leave.

"I need to check in with my parents," I said. "It's dinnertime and I'm supposed to help. They'll be worried about me."

My story worked, because he allowed me to call them. As soon as my stepdad answered, I used the code word in a sentence that I knew he would understand. Once he confirmed my use of the word, he promised to come immediately. He did.

He walked into the house and said, "Sheryl needs to come home now." I walked out of the house with my stepdad and he followed me home in his car. As soon as I walked into our home I realized my mom had been drinking. That was a bad sign. It meant she was angry about something and it usually pertained to my stepdad. It was a pattern I learned to recognize after I moved in with them. It wasn't like it was a daily occurrence, but I quickly learned when Mom was drinking, it was best to steer clear of her. Even when her anger was directed at someone else, I never wanted to be between her and whoever she was mad at.

I ran to my room crying. I was scared. I felt alone. I didn't know what to do. I kept playing the entire day over and over in my head, asking myself what I could have done differently; what did I say to trigger his anger towards me? Did I deserve his ring? The tears he shed made me feel that deep down he was sorry and didn't mean all of the things he said and had done. I felt alone, confused and…guilty.

Within an hour he called me. He said he wanted to give me the ring back (he obviously didn't really swallow it). He declared how much he loved me and needed me; that I was the best thing in the world for him. Since I felt his outburst must have been my fault, I was anxious to return to him and fix the situation.

I bravely went downstairs and told my mom, "He called. He needs me. I need to go to him so we can work this out."

She didn't stop me. She didn't question me. I was surprised that neither my mom nor stepdad seemed concerned that I had just used our family code word, and now I was returning to the person whom I needed to be rescued from not an hour earlier. When I returned later that night no one asked me any questions and nothing else was said about that day.

A few months later my mom and stepdad wanted to look for a smaller, less expensive place to live. I was a few months shy of graduating high school. With their impending move, and the fact that we were engaged, they encouraged us to live together. We were both a little apprehensive at first. The reality of our own apartment seemed overwhelming. In the end, we decided to do it. It didn't seem like all that big a change. He had already been staying with us, sometimes for weeks at a time, because he didn't have consistent living arrangements. I planned on working full time after I graduated, so if we moved in together we figured it would also help him keep an apartment. I allowed his problems to become my problems.

We got our first apartment together in the spring of 1984. Things were moving fast; too fast. I wasn't worried what my friends thought about our living arrangement. By this time most of my friends had slowly disappeared from my daily routine. Our relationship was so exclusive that I rarely had time for any other socializing or girlfriend time. As we got closer and closer, my world grew smaller and smaller.

Almost two months after we moved into our apartment, my mom and stepdad mentioned they were going to go to Reno. They offered to take us along. They would pay for everything, including a limo, if we wanted to get married now. Even though we were engaged and had talked about an August wedding, we had not set a date nor made any plans.

Like most girls I had always dreamed of a wedding with my dad walking me down the aisle. I didn't think my dream would be a reality. My dad had allowed me back into his life a year after I left his house, but I did something else to make him mad and he was not speaking to me again. Even though I wanted him to be a part of this day I decided not to tell him until afterward.

I was hopeful that marriage might make my relationship with my fiancé better. My soon-to-be husband was always questioning my love for him, and jealous of my past relationships. I believed saying my vows to him would prove once and for all my love and loyalty to him.

I believe we were looking at marriage as the answer to all the issues each of us had; loss, heartache, emptiness, shame, guilt and disappointment. Both of us, at a very young age, dreamed of being married to someone, as if that held a magic key towards healing and wholeness.

We said our vows and became man and wife on May 27,

1984. A few weeks later I graduated high school. Plenty of people at school, both my peers and my teachers, wanted to know if I was pregnant. I was not. But secretly I wished I was.

What I Know Now

Red flags usually never change color.

I am not responsible for other people's choices, their past or their issues.

You should never feel fear in any relationship.

Do not marry in the hopes of changing someone, proving your love and loyalty to them, or because of pressure from circumstances or people.

Strands of Hope

1. We have all, at one time or another, ignored red flags. Are there any red flags in your life currently that you may be choosing to ignore?

2. Consider how these verses can represent *not* ignoring red flags in our life: Proverbs 27:12, Proverbs 22:24-25 and Proverbs 4:14-15.

3. What are the differences in encouraging someone and taking responsibility for their choices? What is one piece of advice you would share with a friend you see falling into a pattern of taking responsibility for others' choices.

4. If you recognize you have an unhealthy fear in a relationship, what is one proactive positive step you are willing to take to change this relationship?

5. As believers in Christ, we are not bound by generational sins and curses from our parents or ancestors (whether it's addictions, abuse, or any other detrimental lifestyle choice or behavior). We have a

choice. We are responsible for our own behavior and choices. Read 2 Corinthians 5:17-21.

Chapter 8

The Beating

When I am afraid, I will put my trust in You. In God,
whose word I praise, In God I have put my trust; I shall
not be afraid. What can mere man do to me?

Psalm 56:3-4

Just months after using the family code word to be
rescued, I found myself in yet another situation from
which I needed to be rescued. My husband and I had
gone to a friend's house for a party. Everyone was over 21
years old except the two of us. I was not drinking. He was -
and he seemed to get drunker by the minute. I started feeling
anxious. I knew there was a line in his drinking, and once he
crossed it he became unreasonably angry, and got verbally
and physically abusive. I could tell he wasn't far from that
line.

Some of our other friends also noticed his rapidly shifting
mood and convinced him to go outside for some fresh air.
We walked with him and tried to get him to lighten up, but it
wasn't working. He started ranting about his father, who was
an alcoholic and drug addict, and who had been in and out
of jail most of his life. He ranted about his mother, who
died when he was still a young child. He ranted about the
abuse he suffered at the hands of the foster homes he was
placed in until his father was released from jail.

The more he raged about his life, the more our friends
backed away and left. A police car drove passed us and
looked us over. Within minutes the car drove past again. I
purposely slowed down until I was behind my husband's

back, and quietly flagged down the officer.

I was ashamed. I knew this would likely mean trouble for my husband, but I was scared he would get behind the wheel of the car and drive. He was having a hard enough time walking! I didn't want to drive because, according to him, I drove to slow or too fast, or did not get over quick enough, or let too many people cut in front of me. He once became angry with me because I put the visor down to shield my eyes from the sun - he shoved the visor back into place. Just thinking about driving him home caused fear to shoot throughout my body.

The officer pulled over. "Is everything okay," he asked.

Everything was obviously *not* okay. My husband got belligerent and angry. The officer gave him the choice to calm down or go to jail, but my husband continued with his angry outburst, only this time it was directed at the officer. That was a mistake. He was arrested and taken to jail.

The officer gave me the information I needed to bail him out of jail. I was an hour away from home and I was afraid to go to the county jail alone. No one at the party wanted to get involved. They encouraged me to call someone else to help me. I called my mom and stepdad and they came to get me.

We decided that my mom and I would drive back to their home while my stepdad went to the jail to get my husband. After a few hours we were all back at my mom's home. When my husband walked in, he looked humbled and tired. We started for the car and my stepdad followed us to make sure he was okay to drive.

As soon as we got in the car my husband's humble, tired disposition morphed back into the same anger from earlier in the evening, and venom came spewing from him. My heart began racing. I felt extreme nausea. It seemed as if fear itself was breathing down on me.

I tried to talk calmly. I assured him that I called my parents to get him out of jail as soon as I could. "It's alright now," I told him. "You are home."

He was furious with the officer who arrested him. I felt a small sense of relief that he had no idea I was the one who flagged the officer down. The closer we got to home, the madder he grew, and the more anxious I felt. I actually feared for my life.

My stepdad had followed us to make sure we got to our apartment safely. I fully intended to use our family code word so he would rescue me from this dangerous situation. Unfortunately, my stepdad didn't get out of his car. He only waved good bye as my husband smiled and shouted, "Thanks."

We entered the apartment and I reached to turn the light.

"No!" he shouted. "No lights!"

He shoved me down into our big living room chair, placed his knees on my arms so I couldn't move and began punching my face. When the first blow hit, I remember my whole head being flung viciously to the side. I literally saw stars.

I was terrified! I lost count of how many times he punched me, but eventually the beating stopped. He eventually seemed to come to his senses and realize what he was doing. He leaped up and ran to the bedroom weeping and crying out, "I hit my wife. I can't believe I just hit my wife!"

As odd as it sounds, I tried to comfort him. I went to him and told him I was okay. Instead of showing the remorse I expected, he pushed me down on the bed, sat on my chest and arms, and started pulling my hair and slapping my face. I could hardly breathe. I thought I was going to die.

Silently I prayed, "God please let me live." But somehow, out loud, I managed to scream, "Stop! Stop it!"

Whether in response to my screams or my prayers, he emerged from his frenzy long enough to get off me. He collapsed on the floor next to the bed and cried. I was crying too - because I was terrified that I wouldn't live to see the light of day.

I stumbled to the bathroom and looked at myself in the mirror. My face was battered and bruised, completely swollen and bloody. Then I saw his face in the mirror. He was standing behind me.

"Look what I have done to you," he whined.

I tried to comfort him again, telling him I loved him and I would be fine, but on the inside was was praying, "Lord, please, just let him pass out so I can escape. I promise I will follow You if you just let me live."

I was confused, and racked with guilt. I thought maybe I deserved this beating. After all, I was the one who flagged down the police officer. I didn't even consider that this incident might be my husband's fault; a result of the choices he had made; that his issues were bigger than me and had nothing at all to do with me.

A short time later he passed out. I knew I needed to leave, but I was scared. If he woke up and realized I was trying to leave, I was afraid he would kill me.

Somehow I summoned up the courage to try. I moved as quietly as possible, and thankfully, he stayed asleep. I made it outside, ran to a neighbor's bedroom and began banging on their window. They pulled back their curtains, saw my distressed state and immediately let me in their apartment. I finally felt safe, but everything in me suddenly fell apart. I began to sob and shake as if I would never stop.

When I managed to regain my composure, I called my mom and stepdad. They came to get me at once, and the next morning they took me to a doctor. A thorough examination revealed I had suffered no broken bones, but my body was swollen, covered in bruises, welts and cuts. I was in a lot of pain. I felt like I had been used as a punching bag.

The entire time my mom helped care for me, tending my bruises and cuts, she never suggested that I should leave my husband. She didn't encourage me to file charges against him, and she didn't suggest that I move back in with them. She didn't even suggest that I should consider seeking counseling or any kind of help. In fact, she didn't offer any advice at all. I assumed it was just par for the course in marriage. It was as if she was afraid to tell me what to do. I know she loved and cared about me, but she gave me no guidance whatsoever.

Two days passed before my husband called. He sounded devastated, sad and depressed. He promised he would never drink again and he would go to a men's counselor. He vowed to do whatever he needed to do to get me home again. He wanted me back. He loved me. But he didn't apologize. He never took responsibility for his actions. He insisted it was all that police officer's fault, which in turn made me feel guilty.

I was confused. I looked in the mirror at my swollen and bruised face, and thought of how much he needed me. I was very aware of the violence that could erupt from him, but I also felt responsible for him. I never considered living on my own; I didn't feel capable of doing so and was too afraid to try. I didn't want to live with my mom and stepdad, and even if I did their new apartment was too small. There was no room for me. Going back to my dad's house wasn't an option. We were back on speaking terms, but his drinking

45

was getting worse and he and his wife were going through a divorce.

I wanted to believe my husband loved me and would change, but I wasn't ready to give him an immediate answer about whether I would return home to him or not. Within a few hours he called again. He told me how broken and depressed he was, how he was scared to live without me, how desperate he was. He said he threw out all of the medicine we had in the house, because he couldn't trust himself not to do something drastic if I decided to not come back to him.

More guilt piled down on my shoulders. I not only felt responsible for creating the situation by flagging down the officer, but I now felt responsible for his safety.

I went back. I hoped and prayed things would get better. Out of sheer curiosity, I checked all the medications in the house. They were all exactly where they had been all along. He had lied, but it was nothing I could use to my advantage. My bruises had not yet healed, and I wasn't ready for another confrontation. Instead, I continued on in the same strange pattern of feeling an unhealthy combination of love and fear for my husband.

To his credit, he did go to a men's counselor, and he worked on his anger issues as well as issues he had with his father. Unfortunately, it didn't last. He stopped going to his counseling appointments after a few short weeks. He thought he was better, that he could control his emotions.

For my part, I was struggling with my own emotions for him. I felt he had a love-hate relationship with me. There were times that he seemed to love me, when he was kind and tender towards me, when he would shower me with gifts and attention. At other times it seemed he hated me. Nothing I did was right, nothing I said pleased him. My clothes were wrong, the way I cleaned was wrong, my weight was wrong, even the way I ate my food irritated him.

I determined in my heart to do whatever I could to please him and simply hope for the best. I didn't feel I had any other choice.

What I Know Now

Once again, I am not responsible for other people's choices or behaviors.

There are many red flags or warning signs of an abusive relationship. Here are eight that should not be ignored:

Pushes for a quick and exclusive relationship
Jealous/possessive
Blames others for problems or mistakes
Makes others feel responsible for their feelings or choices
Unrealistic expectations
Angers easily - leaves you feeling like you are walking on egg shells
Has a history of abusing others or animals
Uses words, facial expressions or physical violence to intimidate you

It is important to recognize that without intensive therapy to get to the root of the problem, the abuser will continue to abuse. There is *never* a reason for abusing someone or accepting abusive behavior.

If you or someone you know is in an abusive relationship it is important to seek help immediately. There are many resources available, including the National Domestic Violence Hotline at 1-800-799-7233 or www.ndvh.org.

Strands of Hope

1. Most people in unhealthy or abusive relationships do not recognize they are in such a relationship until they are out. Why do you think this happens?

2. Read Psalm 33:20. Find a picture or draw a picture of something that represents "God is my shield" as a visual for you to *see* when you need reminders of God's help, power and shield about you.

3. Just as we are not responsible for other people's choices or behavior; no one is responsible for your choices or behavior. Is there an area in your life where you're placing responsibility on others for your choices or behavior?

4. The first step toward wholeness and freedom is acknowledgement. The second step is action. If you have an unhealthy pattern in making others responsible for your choices and behavior, what is one thing you can begin to work on to take responsibility for your choices and behavior?

5. Read Psalm 56:8-11. God is attentive to every aspect of your life. What is one area where you feel God is not being attentive in this particular season of your life? Encourage someone this week that God *is* aware and bigger than the season they are in.

CHAPTER 9

SECRETS

Out of the depths I cry to you, O Lord; O Lord, hear my voice. Let your ears be attentive to my cry for mercy. If you, O Lord, kept a record of sins, O Lord, who could stand? But with you there is forgiveness; therefore you are feared.

Psalm 130:1-4

Shortly after the beating, I learned I was pregnant for the second time. I had a secret. My husband didn't know I had stopped taking birth control pills. I wanted a baby. I felt in my heart a baby would soften my husband. I thought a baby would make us a happy family, that it would complete us. I was excited to tell him the news. I assumed he would be just as happy as I was.

I was wrong.

He wasn't happy. He wasn't excited. He was angry. He wasn't ready to be a father, he said. He didn't want to take care of a child at this time in his life, he said. He never said if I decided to keep the baby that I would be on my own, but I sure felt like that's what he meant.

I cried. I begged him to reconsider, but his mind was made up. He had no intention of being a father. My mom and stepdad sided with him. They told me keeping the baby shouldn't even be an option.

My husband wanted me to get an abortion. Since he showed no interest in coming to the appointment with me, my mom and stepdad stepped in. I was devastated and heartbroken. I cried and begged God to please forgive me. Not only was I losing what I wanted, but I was about to abort my second child. I still felt abortion was wrong, but once again I didn't feel as if I had any other choice.

As my mom and stepdad drove me to the appointment, I sat in the back seat and wept hot, angry tears. I was mad at my husband and I was mad at my mom and stepdad for taking his side. I wanted this baby. I planned for this baby. And now, once again, it seemed like I was put in the position of having to please everyone else. My husband never knew about the first abortion and no one knew that I purposely tried to become pregnant this time. Once again I made the wrong decision. I was 18 years old when I had my second abortion. I was left feeling guilty and ashamed. My scarlet cord continued to thicken.

Although I worked full time as a receptionist, I didn't feel secure enough financially or emotionally to consider life on my own and certainly not as a single mother. I kept my secret, my shame and my pain private. My husband and I never talked about the pregnancy or the abortion again. Once it happened everything was swept promptly under my rug.

Life moved along slowly and insignificantly for a while. I didn't suffer another beating at my husband's hand, at least not as severe as that first one, but the fear was ever-present. He would still erupt in anger. Sometimes that anger was directed at me, sometimes it was completely unrelated to me, but I always feared the consequences of his wrath. He did things like grab my wrists and hold them firmly, or push me against a wall and put his forearm against my throat. Sometimes he'd harshly poke me in the chest, or shout and curse at me. If I had a facial expression that he disapproved of, he would command me to "wipe that look off your face!" The only emotion he would accept from me was love and devotion. I felt like a robot; no emotions, no feelings. I tried to keep my focus on anything and everything that would bring peace in our relationship.

His anger and intimidation was not reserved only for me. He enjoyed intimidating others as well. He never thought twice about lying. He'd falsely brag that he was involved in law enforcement or that he had "connections." He enjoyed approaching strangers on the beach in the middle of the night and acting as if they were breaking a law, and that he was there to enforce it. He always won. Few people ever challenged him. He wanted power. He knew how to dominate and intimidate people into doing what he wanted them to do, or believing what he wanted to them to believe.

What I Know Now

Secrets are not usually good. If you feel you have to deliberately go behind someone's back to get what you want, pray through your motives and talk to someone who can help you work through the issues.

A baby will not make you into a family. There are many wonderful reasons to have a baby, but trying to improve your relationship, or change your spouse into someone they are not, isn't one of them. If changes need to occur in your marriage, family or relationships, I urge you to prayerfully consider talking things over with your spouse and possibly set up a counseling appointment before you try to manipulate the situation on your own by getting pregnant.

I have forgiven myself as well as everyone involved. I have also accepted forgiveness from God. But this did not happen overnight. It was a process for me. I wish I had a *forgiveness eraser*, but I don't. I will always remember, and I will always have regret.

If you have had an abortion, please know there is forgiveness available to you. Read Ephesians 1:7 - "*In Him we have redemption through His blood, the forgiveness of our trespasses, according to the riches of His grace."*

Strands of Hope

1. What is the difference in "good" secrets and "bad" secrets?

2. Have you ever intentionally done something in hopes of changing someone or trying to control a situation on your own? If so what was the outcome?

3. How can you begin to let go of what you think is best and begin to trust God's plan and purpose for your life? Read Psalms 119:15-16.

4. Sometimes it is easier to forgive others before we forgive ourselves. If we can accept that God, in His grace and mercy, forgives us, it is possible to begin the journey of self-forgiveness. Read Psalm 103:12, Isaiah 44:22, and Ephesians 1:7.

5. Regrets are part of life and growing. We can however, move forward in our regrets. Is there something you regret that you are not allowing yourself to move forward with?

CHAPTER 10

THE ACCUSATION

The Lord also will be a stronghold for the oppressed, A stronghold in times of trouble; And those who know Your name will put their trust in You, For You, O Lord, have not forsaken those who seek You.

Psalm 9:9-10

After the abortion, things seemed to calm down in our relationship. He had not had a drink in a while and seemed to be trying to control his anger, but I still felt like I was walking on egg shells. I tried hard to please him and to avoid doing anything that might set him off.

We both worked full time and took a community college class together. My husband joined a men's softball team and met a guy named Mark. They quickly became friends, which led to a life long friendship between myself and Mark's wife Lisa. Mark and Lisa were newlyweds, as we were. The difference was, they were Christians.

When they invited us to church with them, I was thrilled. Although I had been praying that God would open a door for us to go to church, I had kept my relationship with God secret from my husband. We never discussed religion or anything spiritual. I saw this as an opportunity to tell him what I believed and that I had accepted Christ while in high school. After only a few short weeks of attending church at The Home Church in Campbell, California, my husband accepted Christ. When he raised his hand during the altar call to accept Christ, Mark, Lisa and I all cried. Mark even gave him his Bible.

53

For a while he was on fire for Christ. We went to church regularly. He seemed humbled by recognizing the reality of what Christ had done for him. Not long after my husband accepted Christ, we joined the church; and within a few months of joining the church, he became a deacon. Our life was changing for the better. His drinking episodes became almost non-existent. He was calmer, and he seemed to have his temper under control.

Still, I couldn't shake the need to be *on guard* all the time. I loved him and feared him at the same time. My stomach was always in a knot, but outwardly I kept smiling, loving and hoping.

Another positive of this time was my dad had started talking to me again. We lived an hour away from each other, and on occasion we would drive to see him and my three youngest siblings. Dad was going through an emotionally hard time: his mother had unexpectedly passed away while she and my grandfather were out-of-state visiting family in Alabama; Dad was in the middle of his divorce; and he was struggling to raise my three younger siblings as a single father.

We took turns having the kids spend weekends with us. My younger sister Shelli spent a lot more time with us than any of the others. She and I were very close, although I am seven years her senior. We were planning to take her camping with us when my dad called to tell me he had something very important to talk to me about, but not to tell my husband.

I didn't know what to expect. I had no idea if this was good news or bad. At first I thought he must have some terrible disease or illness. I told my husband, in part because I was worried and I couldn't keep my concern or emotion inside, but also because I was afraid if I took off work early to meet my dad, and my husband tried to contact me at work and I wasn't where I was supposed to be, there would be trouble.

My husband was concerned and a little anxious, but also very calm. I took off early from work the next day and met my dad and sister at our apartment.

We all sat down on the couch, but my dad got up and started pacing. It was obvious that he and my sister had been crying. I knew whatever it was, it was going to be bad, but nothing could have prepared me for the news they were about to share.

Finally, my dad sat back down on the couch between my sister and me. He wept as he told me that my husband had been molesting my sister.

I grew light headed, as if I might faint at any moment. My heart ached. I thought it might pound its way out of my chest. I was confused and scared.

My dad insisted that I leave with them right then. In an almost robotic state I grabbed my purse and we left.

No one said much on that drive to my grandfather's house. Mostly we all just cried. I was sickened by the things my dad told me that my husband had done to my younger sister. I felt guilty that I had not protected my sister. I was in shock.

I called my husband and told him what my dad had said. He adamantly denied the accusations and proclaimed his innocence. He was calm and reassuring. I was confused. I didn't think my sister would lie or make this up, but at the same time, my husband was strongly calmly denying the claim.

I was in turmoil. I truly did not know what to believe. I felt trapped. Whatever way I decided to believe, I was going to hurt someone I loved, and nothing would ever be the same again.

After much heartache, I made the decision to go home to my husband. He wanted me there and I didn't want to believe my sister's accusations could be true. I had also suspected I was pregnant - we were now both on the same page and agreed it was time to start a family. Even as I made this choice, I struggled with guilt and shame. What if he really did do the things my sister accused him of? But if I was pregnant and chose to leave him, I was afraid I would be forced through another abortion, and I couldn't take that idea. The decision to go home made the weight of my scarlet cord feel heavier than it had felt in a long time.

My dad responded to my decision by cutting off all contact between me and my siblings. He filed molestation charges against my husband. I understood his motivations, but it was still an incredibly painful process. Once the charges were filed, things progressed quickly. There were numerous interviews and conversations with the police. My husband told me that he took and passed a lie detector test. I kept looking for irrefutable evidence of his innocence.

Could he have done this? Was there anything that had happened in the past that was a red flag? There was one incident, but at the time I was too scared to tell anyone about it. I mentioned earlier that it was not unusual for me to share my bed with one of my younger siblings. One night, when my 14 year-old sister was staying the weekend with us, I didn't think twice about having her in my bed. It was pure innocence on my part. Something woke me that night and I saw my husband reaching over me towards her.

"What are you doing?" I said.

He became very angry, cursed at me, and ordered me to, "Go back to sleep!"

This invoked fear in me, as he had not displayed this kind of anger towards me in a while. I was scared of what he might do to me, and I certainly did not want him to harm my sister. I started to second-guess myself. Perhaps I didn't really see what I thought I saw. Perhaps I was wrong. But, if I was wrong, why did he became so angry?

I rolled over towards my sister and closed my eyes, but I didn't sleep the rest of that night. When morning finally came, no one said a word about it. I foolishly never even questioned my sister about it. This particular incident was not listed in the police report, but it served to make my confusion worse. My husband continued to maintain his innocence. My sister continued to accuse him. I wanted undeniable proof, one way or the other.

The months worn on with no communication from my dad or siblings. My stepmom eventually called to tell me that my dad had made a decision to move. Their divorce was final, and he and my grandfather wanted to move back *home* to Alabama. In the midst of all that was going on in this terrible situation I had a moment of hope - as I had suspected, I was pregnant. While I was ecstatic about being pregnant and longing to be a mother it was emotionally challenging. My dad had already missed out on my wedding; now he was going to miss out on the birth of my baby, his first grandchild.

The investigations against my husband ground to a halt. We weren't sure why. The police just stopped coming. My husband didn't want to ask, "Why?" He was just happy he was no longer being questioned. I kept my questions to myself. Did the investigations stop because he was found innocent, or was there just a lack of evidence? Did they stop because my dad moved to another state? Were the charges dropped? Where was the truth? I had no answers, other than to march forward in life, shoving even more things under my rug.

It would be several months before I had a chance to see my brother and two sisters again, just before they were to move.

I was seven-months pregnant at that time. My stepmom was about to get married again, and she was determined to bring peace between my sister and me. She arranged our meeting without my dad's knowledge.

As I arrived at the destination I saw my three siblings and felt a rush of conflicting emotions. My sister and I stood before one another, looking uncomfortable, feeling even more uncomfortable. We embraced, and I could feel the pain within her as we pulled away. I battled with my emotions - guilt, doubt, anxiousness, anger and even fear warred for dominance. My emotions weren't directed at my sister, but at the entire situation.

I loved my sister and I felt I had betrayed her for my selfish desires. I chose to stay with my husband to try to make my dream of a family come true at her expense. I had wanted to believe him as he continued to deny the charges. I desperately wanted this baby and felt the only way to keep the baby would be to stay with him. My husband was more loving and tender towards me since my sister's accusation. His angry outburst were dwindling. He began saying kind things to me and seemed happy that we were going to have a baby. We attended church regularly and he read his Bible and prayed with me.

My sister and I were not necessarily encouraged to talk about the accusation; only to make peace. It appeared we had. It would take almost 25 years for us to talk about this again and for me to ask her direct questions, to find the answers that I needed, to ask her to forgive me, to forgive myself, and to move forward.

What I Know Now

The word *molest* means to bother, interfere with or annoy; to make indecent sexual advances; to assault sexually.

My response to the situation with my sister was affected by

Post Traumatic Stress Disorder and I was in a fight, flight or freeze mode.

During most of my marriage I stayed in the freeze or fight mode, although, my fight mode was not as most would think of the word. My fight mode was trying to stay one step ahead, protecting myself or those close to me - at times even protecting my husband. I responded the only way I knew how at the time.

If you or someone you know is being sexually abused, please tell a trusted adult and contact your local law enforcement.

Strands of Hope

1. Have you ever received life changing news (good or bad) that you were not expecting? How did you handle it?

2. Read Psalm 34:18-19. When we are in the midst of feeling a loss, heart break, or grief it's easy to lose focus and begin to feel alone. During these times we need to allow ourselves to cry out to the Lord and draw nearer to Him.

3. Is there a situation in your life (past or present) where you allowed yourself to "make peace" without confronting the details?

4. Forgiveness is powerful whether it's asking forgiveness, offering forgiveness or being able to forgive yourself. Three important facts to remember with forgiveness:

    • Forgiveness doesn't mean what was done or said is now "okay" or even acceptable.
    • Forgiveness doesn't mean the other person has to acknowledge anything; it's not about them it's about you.

- Forgiveness is an act *and* a process.

5. When we choose to deny something happened, or refuse to seek answers to questions we may not want the answers to, we open the door for the enemy to keep us in bondage to that situation or person. Read 2 Timothy 1:7 and Isaiah 43:1-2. Allow these scriptures to encourage you the next time you find yourself wanting to deny, hide or ignore a situation that needs acknowledgement or confrontation.

CHAPTER 11

HAPPINESS AND DYSFUNCTION

For the mountains may be removed and the hills may shake, But My loving-kindness will not be removed from you, And My covenant of peace will not be shaken, Says the Lord who has compassion on you.

Isaiah 54:10

October 1988 was one of the most special times of my life! My daughter Lauren was born. Being a mom was a dream come true for me. I instantly fell in love with my sweet baby girl. I had never known the true power of love until the very moment that I held her for the first time and looked into her eyes. My husband seemed to beam with pride and joy when she was born. The moment he cut her umbilical cord I saw something different in his eyes. He wanted to be the father he never had. I was overjoyed with the birth of my daughter, but I also had a deep sadness inside of my heart. I longed for my dad and family to share in this moment with me.

A year after my daughter was born I received the call I had been praying for. I could hardly contain myself when I answered the phone and heard his voice: "Sheryl, this is Dad."

I missed my dad and my brother and sisters. I knew he had finally sold both his house and my grandfather's house, which meant they would be moving soon. I wanted him to be a part of my life again. With his call I was eager and willing to push everything deeper under the rug than ever before, just to have my dad back in my life again. I wasn't

61

sure if my husband would agree to let me go and say goodbye. He did, but he told me I had to do it during the week while he was at work, which meant I had to take Lauren and the four-year-old little girl I was babysitting with me.

I was excited to see my family again, but I was also anxious. I wasn't sure if my dad would try to convince me to move with him to Alabama. I knew this might be the last time I'd see my dad, grandfather and siblings, since they were moving so far away. We certainly couldn't afford airplane tickets, and even if we could, I didn't think my husband would be willing to let me go with Lauren.

Once we arrived at my grandfather's home, my dad and grandfather came outside to greet us. When Dad walked up to me we hugged each other and cried. Everyone loved Lauren. I took photos of Lauren with my dad and grandfather. I have a very special picture that my grandfather took of my dad and me together, smiling and hugging as if nothing had happened.

No one said a word about my husband or the accusations. Nothing was said about me moving to Alabama with them. We went about our conversation as if the past two years didn't exist - except that we never mention *his name* and managed to talk around anything that had to do with *him*.

My dad generously offered to pay airfare for Lauren and me to come and visit him each summer. I was thrilled, and hoped that my husband would agree to these visits - particularly since my dad was the one footing the bill.

When it was time to leave, I tried to put on my brave face. I kept my tears in check and refused to let them fall. I made it until I turned the key to start the van. My tears flowed quietly and softy as I sat in the front seat and made the hour-long drive home. I forced myself to stop crying as I took the exit off the freeway that led to my home. I once again buried my feelings deep inside.

Things at home had settled down. We had a baby, and we had taken custody of my husband's 13-year-old brother. He came to live with us just as all of the controversy with my sister started happening. I was happy to have him live with us, not because I thought it was in his best interests, but for safety's sake. I wanted someone else in our home with me…just in case. As it turned out, it also turned out to be the best for my young brother-in-law. He had no stability or discipline while living with his mother, and his father continued to battle with drugs and alcohol. Under our care, he stayed in school and out of trouble.

My husband had grown to enjoy the image of being a "good guy." He wanted people to see him as a provider, a father, a good husband and even a Christian, and he worked hard to maintain that image. We went to church as a family each Sunday, he kept his temper under control and he was positive and encouraging - for a while. But slowly, his old demons crept back in.

I started seeing the same old behaviors and patterns. He'd act like he loved me and hated me all at the same time. At times he'd show me his tender side, shower me with gifts, tell me how much he loved me and needed me. He was a great charmer. At other times he intentionally destroyed my self-confidence and self-esteem with negative comments about me, my body or how I did or did not do something correctly or to his liking. That my perceptions of my own self-worth were already so low only made it easier for me to believe his negative comments. Little by little he filled me with self-doubt which created a greater lack of self-confidence. He called me *vanilla* - boring, and predictable, while he was *rocky road* - spontaneous and adventurous.

Lauren was two years old when he began disappearing for hours at a time. He always came home with some elaborate story about how he rescued someone from a burning car or helped a stranded motorist. I never saw any news reports or acknowledgments for these acts of valor, though I never questioned his stories, I never really believed them either. Sometimes he simply offered no excuse, and I didn't press him. I knew better. He had started drinking again.

His career had finally started to take off, and he started hanging out after work to have drinks with his co-workers. Some nights I wouldn't hear from him until after two o'clock in the morning. I never knew if he was simply hanging out with the guys, seeing someone else or was dead on the side of the road.

Each time he came home I was relieved he was alive, but inside I was furious that he stayed out all night drinking. I kept my anger bottled up, because he would do things to *remind* me of what he was capable of. One night in particular he came home after the bar closed. Although I was awake, I pretended to be asleep. I heard him open his nightstand drawer and take something out. My breath caught in my throat. He always kept a sharp knife in that drawer. My mind raced for the rest of the night as I quietly lay there, wondering what he was planning to do and how I could possibly respond.

When he woke up the next morning, he still had his hand under his pillow. His eyes were blood-shot and I could still smell the alcohol on his breath. He stared straight at me as he pulled the knife from under the pillow.

"Did you put this here?" he asked me.

I was terrified! "No," I responded as calmly as I could. There was no way I could tell him I knew he had grabbed the knife. He thought I was asleep. I felt my best option was to plead ignorance.

He held the knife close to my face. "This is dangerous," he breathed. "I could have accidently killed you last night."

I was scared to death. I didn't know if he was going to shove the blade into my face or stab me in the chest. I answered calmly again, "I did not put the knife there."

He just looked at me for a moment, then sat up, put the knife back in the nightstand drawer, got out of bed, went to bathroom and took a shower. I experienced an odd combination of sheer panic and welcomed relief. I was sweating profusely, my heart was racing and I was sick to my stomach. I needed to keep busy, so I made the bed and then played with Lauren, doing whatever I could to stay out of his way.

After his shower, he dressed and ate breakfast. We went about the day as if the earlier confrontation never took place. My scarlet cord continued to tighten about my neck as I tried desperately to stay one step ahead of my husband each day, hour upon hour, never knowing what to expect.

What I Know Now

While I was grateful to reconcile with my dad and family, it was unfortunate that the situation with my sister was swept under the rug never to be brought up again by my dad or me.

The relationship I had in my marriage was not a healthy loving relationship.

The intimidation that my husband displayed towards me had to do with him and his issues, and nothing to do with me. It is never appropriate to intimidate or bully anyone.

I can now see how I was primed for an abusive relationship. My scarlet cord had already been formed and I was struggling with my own issues of self-worth, self-esteem, self-doubt, guilt, shame and fear. The issues and struggles my husband had, as well as my feelings about myself, set the stage for our dysfunctional, abusive relationship.

I was having panic and anxiety attacks, but didn't realize it. Emotionally I was fighting for my life.

Strands of Hope

1. While reconciliation is an important step towards healing a broken relationship, it also takes courage to address the issues that caused the brokenness in the first place. Read Zechariah 8:16. Is there a situation (past or present) where you need to go back and speak truth in order to bring wholeness back into a relationship?

2. Find two scriptures that speak to God's desire for a healthy marriage relationship.

3. Have you ever felt intimidated or bullied by someone you love? If so how did you handle it?

4. What would you consider the difference in a healthy fear vs. an unhealthy fear, as it relates to relationships with others?

5. Send someone a note of encouragement along with a verse that speaks about trust, wisdom or God's power.

CHAPTER 12

THE AFFAIR

He heals the brokenhearted And binds up their wounds.
Psalm 147:3

With the return of my husband's old patterns, his intense jealousy also returned. He began accusing me of looking at other men or of just thinking about them. He came home at odd times throughout the day, to get a soda or use the bathroom. He said he was out running work errands or on his lunch break; but it appeared to me that he was checking up on me.

I had a home day care business, so I was always at home with children around me. If he was jealous of me, I was also suspicious of him. His behavior grew increasingly secretive. I found motel receipts and photos of another woman - a girl he worked with - in his brief case.

I was devastated. I was furious. And I didn't have the courage to confront him.

I didn't know what to do, but I knew I couldn't keep up the pretense for long. I finally confided in my friend Lisa. We had been friends for a few years, and although I had never confided in her before, she saw right through some of the things that were quietly going on. Together we created a plan for Lauren and me to leave.

On the appointed day, after my husband left for work, Lisa came to get me and Lauren. She was going to take us to her parents' house in Hollister, California, about an hour away. Oddly enough, I remember realizing I had not ironed his shirts for the week. As Lisa was helping me get our suitcases in the car, I said, "I need to iron his shirts before I leave."

She just gave me that look and declared, "No, Sheryl. You are not going to iron his shirts. He can iron his own shirts."

She was right. I left the shirts wrinkled and crumpled on top of the dryer.

I struggled with leaving my young brother-in-law, but it didn't seem right to take him with me. He had a job, a steady girlfriend and was finishing high school. And he wanted to stay. He was rarely home, and when he was he was sleeping or getting ready to leave. I thought he could take care of himself.

Although my husband's affair devastated me, deep down I hoped it was the event that would finally lead to my freedom. I didn't want to be the one to file for a divorce. I was afraid of what he might do to me if he thought the divorce was my idea. He needed to ask for it. If our marriage was ending, I needed it to be *his* decision.

I struggled with guilt for leaving him without telling him where Lauren and I were, but I didn't think I could confront him about his affair and still remain safe if he knew where I was. I thought it might give him the space he needed to plan for a divorce.

I waited five days before I called him. At first he sounded relieved to hear from me, but his relief quickly flashed to anger.

"Never take my daughter away from me like this again," he seethed. "I'm serious. I mean it!"

I believed him. Fear reared its head, forcing me to question my actions and my motives. Internal questions bombarded my mind. Had done the right thing? Maybe I shouldn't have left? Maybe I shouldn't have told him I knew about his infidelity? There was a brief silence between us, then I started crying.

He confessed his affair and told me he was sorry. He said he ended the relationship with his co-worker and wanted me back; that he missed his family.

I felt trapped, like I didn't have a choice except to forgive and go home. I was afraid if I didn't return he would find a way to take my daughter away from me. I thought the best way to protect her was to pack our bags and go back home.

He said he wanted to remain married, and I felt obligated to return and stay in my marriage. But something deep within my heart had already changed towards him. The love I had for him diminished with each lie, motel receipt and photo I saw. I'm not sure how much love remained.

What I Know Now

The affair was not my fault. I am not responsible for other people's choices.

The affair shocked me, but discovering it helped me stop protecting my husband, and to face the reality of who he was and the type of marriage we had.

I was beginning to have courage and see truth, even though I was still fearful of him.

I was still responding to the fight, flight or freeze mode with my PTSD.

Strands of Hope

1. Read Proverbs chapter 2. Which verse(s) inspires you the most and why?

2. Read 2 Samuel chapter 11 and 12.

3. What do you see as a red flag in David's behavior and why?

4. Temptation often comes when we think we can handle it and we begin to allow our spiritual armor to fall off. Consider a time when you *felt* stronger than you were spiritually and fell into temptation.

5. Find a verse that speaks of God's redemptive grace, His unending love and the magnitude of His forgiveness. Write it on an index card and post it somewhere that you will see it.

CHAPTER 13

MY MOM

*Be strong and courageous, do not be afraid, or tremble at
them, for the Lord your God is the one who goes with you
He will not fail you or forsake you.*

Deuteronomy 31:6

S prinkled in throughout my marriage were moments of
what I call *alcoholic outbursts* from my mom. She didn't
drink every day, but when she did she became
argumentative and angry and it usually escalated until there
was some kind of outburst.

After I married she developed the habit of getting drunk,
fighting with my stepdad, then calling me and my husband to
come and get her. We'd bring her to our house where she
stayed until she sobered up and wanted to go home. We
listened as she ranted on and on about my stepdad. She
never made any specific allegation, but always alluded
to…something. In an odd way, it seem to amuse my
husband. He enjoyed this *dance* with my mom, like it was all a
big game to him, trying to decipher what she was hiding or
trying to say. Neither of us could ever figure it out.

Once she sobered up we'd take her home or my stepdad
would come and get her. The next day there would be a
phone call, an apology and a promise not to have any more
alcohol in their house. I knew she always meant it - at least
for a while. After the apology and promise we never talked
about it again. This became a vicious cycle for years. There
was no reason or explanation for her behavior - at least none
that I knew of - and she never sought professional help.

One particular drunken outburst allowed me to begin to see the dysfunction of this pattern. During this call she seemed much more agitated than usual, and a lot more intoxicated. She said she had to tell me something very serious, something very bad. I rushed to get her and bring her to my house. For the next half-hour I did everything I could think of to coax her into telling me whatever it was that had her in such a tizzy.

"Your stepfather is planning to kill the family!" she finally blurted out.

I laughed out loud. I thought she must surely be joking. But she went into graphic detail about his plan, and realized she was serious. While I didn't believe my stepdad would ever do the things she described, she was convinced of his intentions and wanted to escape to a local motel. Once there she wanted more to drink. When I refused to buy her more alcohol, she decided she wanted to go home. I refused to take her. She declared that my stepdad didn't really have a plan to kill us after all. We ended up having an intense argument.

Since I refused to buy more alcohol or take her home, she called the cab and walked out of the motel room. I watched her from the window as she paced the sidewalk, smoking cigarette after cigarette until the cab arrived.

She telephoned the next day. Same song, second verse. She was sorry. There would be no more alcohol in the house. Everything went back normal. We never talked about it again.

After years of training, we were all very good at sweeping things under the rug and never dealing directly with them.

What I Know Now

My mom had a traumatic childhood. Her mother was an

alcoholic and her stepfather was in the army and rarely home. She never knew her biological father. She was neglected and emotionally (and maybe physically) abused as a child. She was one of six children in a very dysfunctional family.

Binge drinking is a form of alcoholism.

Alcoholics are unstable, therefore expecting to have a relationship with someone who struggles with this is challenging.

Alcoholism can be treated, however alcoholic behavior is a choice.

Strands of Hope

1. Do you have a pattern of trying to *rescue* people from their choices?

2. What do you consider healthy boundaries with a loved one who struggles with an addiction?

3. Read Psalm 147:3-5. Write it on an index card and post it somewhere where you will be reminded of this daily.

4. What advice would you give to a friend who is struggling with a parent who has an addiction?

5. Read Psalm 62:5-8. How can you begin to make these verses a part of your daily life?

CHAPTER 14

DIVORCE

For I am the Lord your God, who upholds your right hand, Who says to you, 'Do not fear, I will help you."

Isaiah 41:13

As I struggled to balance my relationship with my mom and my marriage, I tried to keep my head up and just keep moving forward. By this time my husband and I no longer attended church regularly. I continued to pray on my own, but my relationship with Christ was based more in fear and seeking protection, than the relationship that God truly desires with us.

My husband had confessed his affair and told me that he wanted to stay married, to work things out. Eighteen months later his second affair ended our marriage. Ironically, my daughter Lauren was almost five years old - the same age I was when my parents divorced.

Everything unfolded in the summer of 1991. Lauren and I returned from a week-long visit with my dad in Alabama. My husband was always supportive and encouraged me to go each summer. We never talked about what he did while I was gone and he never asked me about my visit. But something was different when we returned home from this particular trip. I couldn't put my finger on it, just...something.

Things had been out of sorts for the past few months prior to the trip, but I resigned myself to thinking this was just the way things were. The day after we had arrived home my husband sat me down in the front room to have a talk.

He told me he didn't want our marriage to end on a bad note with his infidelity, but he was not happy with the life we were living. He wanted a divorce, but he wanted us to remain friends.

I sat silently in total shock; dumbfounded.

I was scared, mad, sad and relieved, all at the same time. I thought it odd that my husband didn't want our marriage to end because of him or his actions, yet it was his drinking, his abuse, his extra-marital affairs that brought us to this precipice. Was he oblivious to all he had been doing since we started dating?

I later found out there was another, much younger woman from work he was involved with. According to him they had not become intimate, but it was obvious he was ready to cross that line. He might not have had physical sex with this woman yet, but he was emotionally having an affair with her and counting down the days until he could act like a "free man."

I felt a small backbone growing.

"If you walk down this road, there is no turning back," I declared. I wanted it clear that this decision was his choice, and once it was made there was no turning back. I determined to stay strong on this point. I knew if I allowed him to come back into my life, I would never be able to move forward.

He agreed.

I was ready to face life on my own with Lauren. He offered to give me physical custody of our daughter, provided he had joint custody rights. I agreed. He offered to provide enough support for me and Lauren to stay in the house we were renting. He would move to a nearby apartment.

He seemed exceptionally calm. There was not a hint of

75

anger in his voice or demeanor. I wasn't sure he took my insistence on no back-and-forth relationship to heart. I was afraid he might grow tired of his *other woman*, and want to come home to me. If that happened, if I opened the door for him to come and go as he pleased in our relationship, I knew I would forever be at his beck and call. I wanted to move forward, but I hurt for our daughter. I knew from my own experience how hard divorce is on children.

The day he moved out I was full of mixed emotions. He was kind and thoughtful. He even hinted at the possibility of *one last time* together. I panicked at the thought. If rejected him, I was afraid he would get angry and possibly abusive. But if I went along with it, I feared opening the door for continuing the relationship. Thankfully he sensed my hesitation. He said he could tell it would probably be too emotional for me, to which I quickly agreed and thanked him for understanding.

After he left with his last load, I laid on the front room floor and cried for hours. My tears were full of anger, resentment, relief, grief, peace and many questions, some of which would be answered in the coming day, and some that never would.

Marriage should be based on trust, honesty and open communication. We had none of that. I wasn't allowed to open any mail unless it was a personal letter addressed to me. He didn't like me around when he was paying bills and we never talked about finances. Six months before he asked for a divorce, he took me to the bank and opened a checking account in my name. He said he wanted me to know how to balance a check book and have some spending money - but he wanted to know what I spent that money on. He told me to keep my checkbook where he could have access to it.

I believe he knew then that he wanted a divorce. In some twisted way he felt obligated to try to help me stand on my own two feet. He knew I had no experience with a check book or with paying bills. I was 27 years old, and this was the first time I had ever had my own checkbook.

I always wondered why he seemed sensitive and secretive about the checkbook and the bills, but I knew better than to ask any questions. Once he moved out I opened some of the bills. I discovered he had racked up close to $30,000 worth of credit card debt, and several of the cards were in my name! To my surprise, he took financial responsibility for all but one card that had a few thousand dollars on it.

My emotions were all over the map. There were moments when I felt strong enough to face the world, and others when I wilted under extreme grief and sorrow. I wanted to be away from him. I was afraid of him. Yet this was the only life I knew. I struggled with the idea of being a divorced woman. I knew God hated divorce. This only added to my scarlet cord.

When I told my dad I was getting a divorce, he was happy.

"It's about time," he declared.

That was all. We still didn't talk about *him*, my sister's accusation, or anything related to my soon-to-be ex-husband. My mom and stepdad wanted to be supportive, and they helped out as much as they could. I thought it was odd that now they were telling me how they never liked or trusted him. My mom told me that after the first beating they were always looking for new bruises on my body, yet they never asked me how my life was going. And if they were looking for the kind of bruises and injuries from the severe beating from years before, those marks were not present. He was careful about the marks he left now.

Most of the marks, other than the ones he occasionally left on my wrists or arms, no one would be able to visibly see. If my mom and stepdad had suspected abuse, I wondered if they would have said or done anything? Was I such a good actor to put on the perfect front? Or were they just accustom to looking the other way?

What I Know Now

All of the emotions I battled were normal. Divorce is difficult no matter the condition of your marriage.

Once my husband opened the door for divorce I responded with the flight mode of PTSD. This gave me the courage I needed to move forward without him.

While the Bible is clear that God hates divorce: Malachi 2:16a "For I hate divorce, says the Lord the God of Israel," it is also clear that the reason He hates divorce is because it breaks the covenant (promise) made at the time of a marriage between two people. Divorce opens the door for remarriage which in itself is not a sin, but it does violate the intended pattern God established when He created one wife for Adam at the beginning of creation.

The Bible tells us there is forgiveness: Acts 13:38-39 "therefore let it be known to you, brethren, that through Him forgiveness of sins is proclaimed to you, and through Him everyone who believes is freed from all things, from which you could not be freed through the Law of Moses".

Strands of Hope

1. What are the three most important qualities that you have, want or need in a marriage relationship?

2. Read Isaiah 58:11 and consider how the Lord has satisfied your desires in the scorched places of your past.

3. Read Isaiah 43:18-19 and do something deliberate to live this scripture out.

4. Is there an area in your life that you lack knowledge which makes you dependent on someone else (i.e.

finances, making decisions, self-control, a skill, etc). Prayerfully consider all of the opportunities that you have to grow in this area. Read James 1:5.

5. What are some things that you would encourage someone whom you suspect is in an abusive relationship?

CHAPTER 15
A SINGLE MOM

*The Lord is near to the brokenhearted And saves those
who are crushed in spirit. Many are the afflictions of the
righteous, But the Lord delivers him out of them all.*

Psalm 34:18-19

Now that I was living on my own I felt overwhelmed,
but I knew I could not rest. I had to be strong for
my daughter. I was in no way prepared to be
independent. I didn't know anything about budgeting, credit
cards, finance charges or paying bills, and was an emotional
wreck from the guilt of not making my marriage work.
Questions plagued my mind constantly. Did I do enough?
Did I give up too soon? Could I have been a better wife?
How will Lauren ultimately be shaped by this decision?
Would divorce really free me from his wrath and the feeling
of walking on egg shells in his presence? Was I even capable
of living on my own?

And I was mad at God. After all, hadn't I put up with
enough from my husband? Shouldn't God have blessed the
marriage for my sake? Why couldn't He just reach down and
make my husband feel differently towards me? Why didn't
He take away my husband's anger and pain? I had followed
all the rules. I did everything I could to please him. I kept his
house clean, ironed his shirts, made his dinner on time, did
the things he wanted and expected...and I took all of the
garbage he dished out on me. He should have loved me. Our
marriage should have been complete. But that's not what
happened.

I didn't want my emotional struggle to negatively impact my daughter. I wanted to do whatever I could to make this change as easy as possible on Lauren. I knew I had to *play nice* with her dad for her sake. That meant including him in certain activities and decisions.

I didn't want to confront him on things that might trigger an angry response, but I was done with his bullying. I determined if he ever physically touched me in an abusive way, I would fight back and I would fight hard. I never had to test my decision. He never touched me again, but I never forgot what he was capable of.

Now that my daughter was a child of divorce I wanted to spare her some of the things I had experienced. I was careful how I spoke about her dad in front of her and to others. In public I went along with his side of the story: *we loved one another but because we were opposite of one another, we no longer wanted to be married; however, we were great friends.* It was a lie, and I hated it, but wanted to spare Lauren the turmoil I went through as a child.

Even though he had moved to his own apartment, he thought nothing of looking through my mail or opening a cupboard or peering into one of my closets. I lived emotionally as if he still lived in my house. I discovered later that women in abusive relationships function differently than women in a loving, trusting marriage. After we were divorced I still found myself on guard, always prepared, for what I don't know.

If you were to read the journals I kept from the beginning of my pregnancy with Lauren until our final separation, you would think our life together was good. The truth is, even then I knew he had no qualms about reading my private journals and correspondence. I had to watch everything I said, did or wrote.

On top of everything else was the overwhelming sense of loneliness, especially on those nights when Lauren was with her dad. She visited him once a week for dinner and spent every other weekend with him. I had never been away from her before.

Within a few months of being single, I began to rebel and ease back into my old habits of seeking out unhealthy relationships, relationships with no depth, no love and no security attached to them. Most were short term and unhealthy.

One such relationship lasted almost nine months, but it was doomed from the start. He was divorced with four children. He affirmed me and genuinely cared about me. For a time he filled the emptiness in my heart, but he was an alcoholic. He was not abusive, but in the end his alcoholism and inability to keep a steady job proved too much for me.

I found myself wondering why I married the man I did and why I felt the way I did about our relationship? I didn't want a repeat of the past nine years, so I stayed away from dominate or controlling personalities, but I was still not making wise choices in the men I dated. I needed help to make sense of all the questions floating around in my mind and heart. I needed a counselor, someone wise and insightful who could help me process my experiences and encourage me to move forward.

I went back to the church my husband and I first attended when he accepted Christ. They offered free counseling and since I no longer had medical insurance and my finances were tight, this seemed like a good option. I set up an appointment and was matched with an older woman in the church. I looked forward to being open and honest with someone who could help me lighten the weight of my scarlet cord.

As I began to unravel my story and feelings I could tell she didn't really understand what was going on within me. She sat and listened, and at the end of our sessions she prayed over me. I went a grand total of twice. While she was a great listener and sincerely prayed for me, she had no advice, wisdom or encouragement for me. I still felt alone and ashamed.

I figured it was probably best to continue to carry it all inside. After all, by now I was used to it.

What I Know Now

I felt like a failure. I had tried with all of my heart to love and serve my husband, but it was never enough. I felt that I let our daughter down. I didn't want her to deal with the same issues that I did as a child of divorced parents.

I recognize now that I was not a failure. I did not fail my marriage or my daughter.

I needed professional counseling; the counseling I received at the time was from a church-trained volunteer. While I feel this type of counseling can serve a purpose in church, I needed a professional who was trained to help me identify areas in my life and help me walk through the process of the divorce and areas of my past.

I was still looking for someone to fill my emotional needs.

Because I was filled with guilt and shame I continued to settle for less than God's best for me.

During this season of my life there are other regrets and choices that I made that I have struggled with. While forgiveness does not come with an eraser, I have finally been able to forgive myself and accept God's forgiveness.

Strands of Hope

1. Is there a time when you *felt* you did all the *right things*

83

and it still didn't work out the way you wanted? How did you deal with the disappointment?

2. Read Hebrews 12:1-2. What can you choose to do differently this week so you can allow yourself to live this verse out?

3. Is there a life skill, concept or wisdom that you wish you had been taught as a child or young adult and you weren't?

4. What advice would you give to someone who is struggling with being angry at God for the outcome of a choice they made?

5. Have you allowed yourself to settle for less than God's best? And if so, what steps can you take to ensure that won't happen again?

CHAPTER 16

MEETING JUNGLE DOUG

But prove yourselves doers of the word, and not merely hearers who delude themselves.

James 1:22

After struggling through almost two years as a divorced woman and single mom, I was beginning to settle into who I was. I tried new things. I ate things that I wanted, just because I wanted to - not because someone else thought I should. I watched movies, read books, painted and listened to music I had never heard before. I experimented with my freedom.

I started listening to a local country music radio station and discovered that I really enjoyed the morning show with Gary Scott Thomas and Jungle Doug. I loved Doug's voice from the very beginning. He sounded like a genuinely nice guy on the radio. He had a great sense of humor and he made me laugh.

I moved from the old house I had shared with my ex-husband in Santa Clara, California, to a small two-bedroom apartment in Sunnyvale. For a while I dated a guy who flew helicopters, but it didn't take long for me to realize *helicopter guy* and I were on two very different paths. We had differing opinions on life's most important topics, one of which was religion. He was an atheist, and while I was not involved in church at the time, I knew there was a God. He was looking to settle down. I wanted to settle down too, but I knew he wasn't the one I wanted to spend the rest of my life with.

Another red flag was his relationship with Lauren. He seemed to care about my daughter, but he wasn't interested in doing things with her. He always looked forward to the the weekend she spent with her father.

One morning as I was listening to the radio while getting ready for work, I heard Jungle Doug say he was going to be at a local business for a radio remote. As the remote broadcast was close by, I thought I would drop by after work. I thought it would be fun, and I was excited to meet the man behind the voice. I was curious about what he looked like, and whether he really was as nice as he seemed on the radio.

After our initial meeting we quickly became friends. I was still dating *helicopter guy* and Doug was involved with several women in non-exclusive relationships. Our conversations and relationship was strictly on a friendship level. But with each conversation we discovered we had a lot in common. He was divorced, like me, but with no children. He was a Christian, but like me, he was not living a life honoring or pleasing to God. Like me, he knew when he was ready to settle down again he wanted it to be a marriage centered on Christ.

I enjoyed being around him. He always made me laugh. He made me feel good about myself.

It didn't take long before friendship started to evolve in to something more. I realized the relationship I was in had no depth and was not going to stand the test of time. I broke up with *helicopter guy* and Doug and I progressed to a dating relationship. Within a few months he ended all of his non-exclusive dating relationships and we became an exclusive couple.

The fact is, I was falling for him; hard! I was physically and emotionally attracted to him. I felt safe around him. I called him my KISA – Knight in Shining Armor. He genuinely cared for, *and liked,* my daughter. He always included her; playing games, reading books and even playing *Barbie* with her. He helped her with homework. I knew the person I married would have to accept Lauren and me as a total package - no ifs, ands or buts. Doug did. Lauren liked and accepted her "Jungle," as she liked to call him, too.

We entered our relationship with lots of emotional and spiritual baggage. Within five months of dating we became engaged and Doug moved in with Lauren and me. Things went well for a while. We both wanted to go to church, but we felt like we should wait until we were married. We knew that sex before marriage was not God's perfect plan. God created sex for pleasure, but that pleasure was intended for the confines of marriage, in a safe, loving, monogamous and committed relationship. We lived as if God had blinders on and could not see the choices we were making, and we continued to live for our own desires.

I was careful not to tell my friend Lisa that Doug had moved in with me. I knew she would be disappointed. She wanted the best for me and was unaware of some of the choices I was making. When Doug and I became engaged I asked Lisa to be a bridesmaid. She was thrilled and agreed, but when she began to suspect we were living together she called and asked me point blank.

I told her the truth. I knew she would be disappointed, but I was glad I no longer had to hide this part of my life from her.

"Sheryl, I love you and I think Doug is a great guy," she said. "I think you both love the Lord, but what you are doing is wrong. I want to be there for you, but I cannot support you like this. I can't be in your wedding. I can't stand up with you."

She was right. I knew she was right. But I wasn't willing to have Doug move out. She followed up that quick conversation up with a letter. I still have that letter to this day, and I use it as part of my testimony. In the letter Lisa told me she loved me, but God can never bless a relationship in sin. She lovingly but firmly challenged me to do the right thing.

I told Doug about the letter. We both knew she was right but we were not worried about God at that time. In our minds, God would come later. I was sad Lisa wouldn't be in the wedding, but I was grateful she would at least be there to celebrate with us.

As the months went by I began to notice changes in Doug. He seemed suddenly distant and unsure. With the date for my bridal shower approaching, he told me he was unsure about getting married. After lots of heartache on my part, we decided to cancel the bridal shower. Unlike the patterns I had always been in, I refused to be quiet and sweep it under the rug. I tried to talk to him, but he was vague and distant. Was this the part Lisa had warned us about, when God would not bless our relationship?

I wanted to go to church. I needed to seek God. Yet once again I was seeking God for protection - not for my physical safety, but for my heart. I still didn't understand that God wanted a relationship with me, that I could come to Him for more than just protection.

I called Doug's best friend, Hans, who I knew was a grounded and respectful Christian, and asked him if Lauren and I could meet him at his church. I knew it was local and Lisa said it was a good church. Hans took Lauren and me to church with him several times. Doug didn't want to come with us; things had come to a standstill in our relationship. He didn't want to move forward, but it seemed he didn't want to completely let go either.

It was confusing, and I felt like an emotional mess. I was disappointed that I allowed myself to let go emotionally and trust him as much as I had. I allowed myself to cross a line that I had barricaded a long time ago. I wanted to be wanted and loved for who I was and I had felt that with Doug - that is until his sudden doubt crept in.

My scarlet cord continued to remind me of my guilt and shame. I felt like a failure and unworthy of finding true love and commitment. Lisa encouraged me to seek counseling. She recommended a wonderful Christian counselor, Dr. Don Phillips. She and her husband had used Dr. Phillips' services when they were struggling through some marital issues years earlier. I asked Doug to come with me. He agreed.

Dr. Phillips opened my eyes to see that my relationship with God needed some major attention. I needed to learn new truths about God; about who He is and who I am in Christ; truths I had not heard or realized before. He also helped me recognize my relationships with men were usually unhealthy. Even though I made sure to stay away from abusive men, I was still putting too much trust and hope in one man. That trust and hope is reserved for God. I began to learn about healthy boundaries and how to let God be the center of my life. I did not need a man to fill this void. God was willing and able.

Although we continued these counseling sessions, Doug still seemed unsure about getting married. I wondered what I had done wrong to make him begin to question *us*. I couldn't understand why he suddenly changed his mind about me. Were all of the cards, notes and words of affirmation lies? Had I been duped again? I thought we were on the same page. His uncertainty seemed to come out of nowhere.

The wedding date was fast approaching, and we decided to do the unthinkable, at least in my mind. We postponed the wedding. He made all the calls. He even stayed at a hotel for a few nights. I couldn't help but wonder how I messed this up. My scarlet cord was hanging tightly around my neck and it was getting heavier by the day.

What I Know Now

Doug and I were putting ourselves and our desires ahead of God.

A pastor once said, "If you want to be covered by the will of God, you must choose to come under the covering and stay there."

I allowed myself to fall back into old patterns and tried to take responsibility for someone else's feelings or problems.

Strands of Hope

1. Have you ever had a confrontation with a friend when you were in the wrong and they were speaking truth into your life? What was the end result?

2. To be honest, even when it's uncomfortable, isn't always easy. Read Proverbs 27:6.

3. Are there areas in your life where you are *pretending* God has blinders on and can't see the sin you are in?

4. Read James 1:22-24.

5. Have you fallen into the trap of being a *hearer* and not a *doer*? What is one step forward you are willing to take towards being a *doer*?

CHAPTER 17

TRUTH

Cast away from you all your transgressions which you have committed and make yourselves a new heart and a new spirit! For why will you die, O house of Israel? "For I have no pleasure in the death of anyone who dies," declares the Lord God. "Therefore, repent and live."

Ezekiel 18:31-32

After months of confusion and the on-again, off-again feeling I was getting from Doug, everything came to a head one night in May of 1996. That night Doug gave me a letter that explained everything. I only read the first few lines. I saw all I needed to see. He admitted to seeing someone else.

I was completely devastated. I literally felt myself snap inside. I was broken.

I ripped the letter to shreds and threw it at him. I vaguely remember calling my mom telling her to come and get Lauren. I had enough sense to know I didn't want her to hear or see whatever might happen next. I took my engagement ring off and threw it as hard as I could at his face. I ran around the apartment grabbing every picture of us I could find and tearing them in half. I pulled his clothes from the closet and threw them on the floor.

Doug tried to calm me down and talk to me. I wasn't interested in calming down *or* talking. I wanted him to know how much he hurt me, and I wanted him to hurt too. I wanted him to feel my pain.

I had let my guard down. I trusted him with all my heart!

The way I was expressing myself was new to me. I was not use to showing my emotions like this. I allowed myself to feel something *and* show it on the outside. My tirade went on for what seemed like hours, but at some point my adrenaline ran out. I was exhausted. I laid down on the bed and fell asleep.

Doug stayed by my side throughout the night. I do not remember the exact details; I just remember waking up and seeing him looking at me and him saying, "I am so sorry. I love you."

I wanted to believe him, but with my history of relationships with men, "sorry" didn't count for much. Apologies didn't guarantee the same action wouldn't happen again. I don't know why but, I said, "I love you, too."

I was confused. I *did* love him. At that moment, I also hated him. I certainly wasn't ready to forgive him. But by admitting, "I love you," I opened the door for forgiveness and freedom - for both of us.

I thought it might be helpful to have Doug tell his story in his own words.

Doug's Story

I spent my senior year of high school in Germany, as an exchange student. It was a great experience for me. I grew a lot during my time in that country. I also met a girl who would later become my wife. We were married for almost five years.

We were total opposites and in the end I think I was trying to marry my awesome experience in Germany through her. I strayed from my marriage and my vows. I became involved with a new chat service on the Internet, where I met a woman. We chatted. We cheated. That relationship spelled the end of my marriage. This behavior of starting a new relationship before ending the existing relationship developed into a recurring pattern.

For the next several years I explored a number of relationships. Each one had something different to offer, but none of them checked all my boxes. One person might be fun, but not pretty; another might be pretty, but not overly bright.

Fast forward to Sheryl. I remember talking to her on the phone; talking about her problems, her relationships and life in general. I was used to assuming the role of 'counselor' when talking to women, especially beautiful women I was attracted to. This had been my lot in life since Jr High. I was always great at talking to the *hotties*, but they were always *hot* for someone else, not a geek boy like me.

I was in the middle of dating the world when I met Sheryl. I wanted to take our relationship slowly, to be her friend. Quite frankly, my 'date plate' was already quite full. At first we talked on the phone, then we finally met in person at Mail Boxes Etc during a radio remote. *Man!* I thought. *She's hot!*

Our first date was Mexican food. It ended with a hug - nothing more.

Sheryl definitely *checked all my boxes*. She was everything I wanted. My mind went straight to, *let's get hooked up, let's get married!* But our testimony is, *God cannot bless sin.* He could not, and did not, bless our living together.

"So," you may ask, "why stray when you have it all?" For me, it was a pattern. Although I was in an exclusive relationship with Sheryl, I would still connect with radio listeners for lunch. Harmless, right? No big deal. But when you put yourself in dangerous situations, when you play with fire, you will get burned. At one lunch, I felt an attraction to another woman. She couldn't hold a candle to Sheryl, but I was still a prisoner to the pattern of my life: I met someone, we clicked, we dated, then I strayed. It's just how my life operated.

I was a jerk to Sheryl; lying about not being sure about getting married, saying *I need time to think, I'll take a drive* only to connect with the other woman. On the other end of the spectrum I was telling the other woman, *Yes, I am breaking up with Sheryl; there will be time for us,* when I really did not want to end my relationship with Sheryl at all.

Finally, God got a message through my thick skull - *"Stop running. Stop running from Me!"*

I knew God had allowed His grace to pour over me during my season of *dating the world.* He had protected me from my own seriously stupid and dangerous behavior, and now He was giving me the woman of my dreams, but He wanted me to follow Him in order to have Sheryl.

I felt awful. I knew I had to come clean to Sheryl, but I was so scared that I would lose her. God had given me the desire of my heart, and if all of my other relationships proved anything it was that I totally *knew* that Sheryl was the best for me. And I knew that I had to stop running from God.

The night I finally had the courage to tell Sheryl everything was the night from Hell, but through all the emotions and all the pain we began a relationship that was blessed by God. Now we stand as a testimony of the truth, and the truth is:

1) God can't bless something done in sin.
2) As long as you have breath, you still have a chance to ask for forgiveness and turn your life around.

Once the truth came out we both took the opportunity to put everything out on the table. We had a chance at a new beginning. This was going to be a new relationship for us in many ways - individually and collectively.

Doug wanted to come completely clean about everything. He said he loved me and was sorry, although those *words* did not have a whole lot of meaning to me at the time - I needed to see it *action*. He was willing to call the counselor and tell him everything. He wanted to go to church with me. He wanted us to have clean slates and make God a part of our relationship.

He took a huge leap of faith by confessing to me. I took a huge leap of faith by allowing him to continue to be in my life. For the first time we prayed together. It was awkward for both of us, but at the same time it was very comforting.

The next day we met with the counselor and things progressed quickly. He helped us walk through this new chapter. We talked openly about everything. We debated if he should move out so we could keep our new vow of abstinence until marriage. We were determined that we would be married as *spiritual* virgins. We decided Doug would stay in the apartment, but he would sleep on the couch. We wanted to do it right this time. We wanted God to be first in our relationship. We wanted God at the head of our home.

As the days passed we realized the temptation to undo our vow of abstinence was growing stronger. Once you open the door to certain behaviors in a relationship, it's hard to close them again. We wanted to start our new beginning with integrity. At our next counseling appointment, we talked to our counselor about getting married sooner.

We married May 22, 1996. Our counselor was an ordained minister, so we asked him if he would be willing to marry us in his office with my best friend Lisa and Doug's best friend Hans by our side. We kept our original date June 9th and used it to renew our vows and share our testimony before family and friends.

During our June 9th ceremony, we played the song *This Time* by David Meece. It's a beautifully written song about second chances and moving forward in life. We wanted everyone who attended our wedding to hear our testimony through this song.

We were originally going to have a bridal party, but everything was different now. We felt that Lauren was supposed to be my only bridal attendant. She was my maid of honor and our flower girl. My dad flew to California from Alabama so he could walk me down the aisle. As Doug entered the room, his mom walked him down the aisle to the song, *Going to the Chapel*. This was not the wedding and reception that we had originally planned. It was now about the family we both had longed for, as the song says, This Time, it was about *second chances with no backward glances* for us.

Our wedding was everything I dreamed of and more. God redeemed not only our relationship, but used it as a catalyst towards a renewed relationship with my dad. We were able to share our testimony with everyone through the wedding ceremony, then we celebrated God's grace and redemption through our reception. It was a party that I imagine was similar to the one the father in the parable threw for his prodigal son! God in His grace and mercy opened His arms to Doug and I as we confessed, repented and moved forward with determination and courage.

What I Know Now

There is freedom in truth, even when the truth hurts.

You cannot *out sin* God's grace, mercy or forgiveness.

God allowed us to almost lose our relationship to gain it.

As hard as it was, Doug's confession was the key turning point in our relationship.

96

God can not be a part of a relationship where He is not invited or included.

Strands of Hope

1. The root of a lot of our sin is pride and selfishness. What can you do to keep these roots from digging deeper into your life?

2. Read Proverbs 15:3 and Jeremiah 23:23-24.

3. Are you holding onto a secret that is hindering your spiritual growth?

4. Is God a part of every relationship you have?

5. Read 1 Peter 2:1-6. Craving comes by experience. What is something you are doing or can do to live this scripture out and place God as a priority in your life?

CHAPTER 18

A NEW LIFE

*Everyone who comes to Me and hears My words and acts
on them, I will show you whom he is like: he is like a
man building a house, who dug deep and laid a
foundation on the rock; and when a flood occurred, the
torrent burst against that house and could not shake it,
because it had been well built. But the one who has heard
and has not acted accordingly, is like a man who built a
house on the ground without any foundation; and the
torrent burst against it and immediately it collapsed, and
the ruin of that house was great.*

Luke 6:47-49

Looking back I can see how quickly things fell into place after we gave our hearts to Christ. That doesn't mean everything was easy. We still had our struggles and challenges. It took a lot of time, commitment and communication to re-build trust. Actions speak louder than words, and part of the commitment we made to one another involved placing boundaries on our interactions with persons of the opposite gender. We still practice these boundaries today. Doug and I love Billy Graham's philosophy of choosing not to go anywhere with a member of the opposite sex alone. There has to be at least one other person present. We respect each other, as well as ourselves, and do not want to put ourselves in compromising situations or give the illusion of anything beyond honor and integrity within our marriage.

We work hard to keep our spiritual armor on. We pray for

each other daily. We talk about everything. I have worked hard at not allowing anything to be swept under the rug. Yes, it can be difficult, but it's important.

As a family we immediately connected with the church I had started attending, Westgate Community Church, in San Jose, California. We went every Sunday. Doug and I knew fellowship with other believers was vital to our spiritual growth, so we joined a small group. Lauren followed our lead and participated in the *Awanas* children's program. She came to accept Christ and chose to be baptized.

I participated in women events at the church. As I began to open up with other women, I saw that even though they all looked perfect on the outside and had the appearance of having it all together, they each had a story as well. I began to see I did not have to be perfect in the eyes of God, nor to these women. I realized for the first time in my life that God wanted me just as I am - scarlet cord and all.

A year and a half after making our commitment to God and our family, Doug heard about a job opportunity for a morning radio show host with a Christian network outside of Nashville, Tennessee. At the time things were quiet with my ex-husband, but I never knew when that would change. I always included him with Lauren's school and church functions, but I still feared him. I was aware of his temper, so I did whatever I had to do to keep him from being angry at me. I had an irrational fear that he would come after me or have someone else do it. I was also concerned that he would try to take Lauren away from me, either through a legal court battle or even by kidnapping her. He had never threatened me with any of this, but I felt he was more than capable to do these things if he wanted.

Still, I still wanted things to be okay for Lauren. I didn't want to put her through the things I endured as a child of divorce.

I was careful not to tell her negative things about her dad. I kept my fears and thoughts inside, tightly wrapped up with a scarlet cord.

Doug inquired about the morning show position, then applied for it. Before we knew it, the Christian radio station in Tennessee was on the phone, offering Doug the job. It was a wonderful opportunity - there was just one catch. The move would put thousands of miles between our family and Lauren's dad. One stipulation in our divorce agreement was that we had to have one another's written permission to take Lauren outside of the state of California. I was hesitant to ask him for that permission. I didn't know what he would say. I was surprised by his response. He seemed genuinely happy for us and gave me both verbal and written permission to take Lauren to live out of state.

Our spiritual growth produced some unexpected side effects. I noticed subtle changes in my relationship with my mom. It seemed the closer we grew to God, the further away she and my stepdad pulled from us. There was a lot that I didn't know or understand about my mom. I began to see patterns in her behavior that confused me.

While we prepared for our move, we found out I was pregnant. To say we were excited is an understatement! Not only were we moving to a new state, but we would have an addition to our family. In the midst of all the hustle and bustle involving the move and the new pregnancy, my mom and stepdad announced that they were also going to move to Tennessee.

I was perplexed, particularly in light of what I felt about them pulling away from us. *They had considered moving to escape the high prices of California*, they explained. *They wanted to retire in an area where prices were more affordable,* they said. Since we were moving to Tennessee, they figured, *why not?* That's where they would settle as well.

Doug moved to Tennessee in February 1998 while Lauren and I stayed in California so she could finish her fourth grade year. Doug came home most weekends. This allowed us a few months to pack and get things organized. During Lauren's spring break she and I flew to Tennessee and we found a town home to rent, a doctor to deliver the baby, a school for Lauren to start in the fall, and we visited a church. Lauren and I officially joined Doug in Tennessee June 1998. The baby was due in August.

Our son Garic entered the world in August 1998. I felt blessed that God allowed me to have another child - a son! Lauren had been anticipating her brother's arrival; she talked to him daily while he was inside my womb. She couldn't wait to hold and cuddle her baby brother. Doug was thrilled at the thought of having a son. He loved Lauren as if she were his very own, but now he had the opportunity to raise and love a child from the very beginning of its life.

I experienced the same over flowing sense of love as when my daughter was born ten years earlier. Words cannot adequately describe how it feels to hold your newborn baby for the first time. The moment Garic arrived and we heard his healthy cry, Doug and I cried too. We kept telling each other, "We have a son! We have a son!"

My dad drove three and a half hours from Alabama to Tennessee to meet his new grandson. I hugged him tightly and thanked him for coming. He hugged me back firmly, smiled and said, "I wasn't missin' out on this one."

After we brought our son home and settled in for our new family life, we made it a priority to get plugged into a good church. We settled on Harpeth Heights Baptist Church, in Nashville. We were active and involved with Sunday service, Sunday school and Wednesday nights. This is where I felt my first calling from God to lead other women. For me, women's ministry has been a labor of love.

I started by leading a Moms in Touch prayer group. Later I led book studies based on the *Bad Girls of the Bible* series by Liz Curtis Higgs. I was intrigued by the title, and once I read the first book, I was hooked. I was overwhelmed by the author's honesty and testimony. I felt connected to her. She was real. She had walked in similar shoes as mine. I related to the women she taught about in the Bible as well. These women suddenly became alive to me. It was a life-changing book and I wanted to share it with anyone who would listen. To my surprise over twenty women signed up to read and discuss *Bad Girls of the Bible*.

With each book we read and discussed it seemed our masks were coming off. This was the first time in my life that I openly shared my testimony. I was in awe at their response. I began seeing my sins not as a scarlet cord around my neck, but as a testimony of God's grace and forgiveness. The scarlet cord became a symbol of the blood of Jesus washing over all of my sins, cleansing me of my guilt, rather than a hangman's noose reminding me of my guilt and shame. This was a huge turning point in my spiritual life. Doug created a similar group for men, where they prayed and studied the Bible. He shared openly about his past. We both recognized the power of taking off the mask and walking in truth.

What I Know Now

Healthy boundaries in a marriage are important. Every couple needs to identify (preferably before you say, *I do*) what your healthy boundaries will be.

Finding a church family and getting involved is important for your spiritual growth.

I was still functioning within PTSD with my ex-husband.

Getting involved with other women at church was a first step in moving forward for me.

Taking the mask off and being real with others is never easy, but it is always rewarding in the end.

Strands of Hope

1. If you have experienced broken trust in a relationship and have reconciled and rebuilt it, what is something you did to move towards reconciliation and healing in that relationship?

2. Confessing is the first step towards reconciliation. Read Proverbs 28:13.

3. Confession, repentance and reconciliation change a relationship. Sometimes the relationship grows deeper and sometimes it comes with forgiveness with a boundary of distance. Is there a time when you have experienced forgiveness with a boundary of distance?

4. Encourage someone who has been a positive role model in your life and who has taken off their mask in spite of their past.

5. Read Ephesians 6:13-18. Write down the things you are currently doing to put on your armor of God. Make another list of things that you can realistically add to this within the next year to deepen your relationship with God and keep your armor strong.

CHAPTER 19

MY DAD

He said to them, "Because of the littleness of your faith;
for truly I say to you, if you have faith the size of a
mustard seed, you will say to this mountain, 'Move from
here to there,' and it will move; and nothing will be
impossible to you."

Matthew 17:20

My dad was an alcoholic. He also suffered from depression. He died unexpectedly in May of 2000. My dad was never treated for either condition, although I'm convinced he suffered from both. I also believe he is healed from all of his afflictions and grief as he now resides in Heaven.

As a young teenager my dad heard Billy Graham preach on the television and made the decision to accept Jesus as his Lord and Savior. Since he didn't have a foundation and didn't pursue a relationship with Jesus, it simply became a belief and not a lifestyle. His parent's grew up in the South where going to church was simply a part of life, but there was not any depth to their faith traditions. Church wasn't a part of their family life once my grandparents married and had children.

My dad was a compassionate man who had a strong belief in family. He was an avid gardener and a wonderful cook. His weakness revolved around confrontations, communication and alcohol. He was not one to overtly show his feelings. He let you know you had disappointed him or hurt his feelings by giving you the silent treatment.

I have very few memories of my dad when he was completely sober. He usually had a beer in his hand by afternoon. Later in life he went straight for the hard stuff, and started first thing in the morning. His last years were filled with severe alcoholism, depression and grief. His mother's untimely death in 1984 was emotionally hard for him. My grandmother had a few health problems, but no one suspected that she would have a heart attack and die. She was out of state on a trip when she died and my dad was devastated that he did not get to say goodbye to her. He was close to both of his parents, but especially to his mother. After her death, his drinking increased.

My grandmother's death, combined with the strained relationship caused by the situation between my ex-husband and younger sister, compelled my dad and grandfather to move back home to Albertville, Alabama. They bought houses within walking distance of each other. In the midst of trying to fill his void with alcohol, my dad started attending church. Every Sunday morning my dad and grandfather drove an hour to attend his cousin's church, Mountain View Baptist Church, in Birmingham. Shortly after they began attending, my dad and grandfather walked the aisle together as they accepted Jesus as their Lord and Savior. I'll never forget the phone call from my dad as he told me of his decision. He was excited. I was overjoyed.

A short time later my grandfather died of lung cancer. My dad spiraled hard and fast into a severe depression. His drinking became even more of a problem. He never considered reaching out for help and certainly wouldn't have accepted intervention. It was easier for him to reach for the bottle.

After my grandfather passed away, my dad continued to go to church for a while and he even made the decision for baptism. He was proud of this decision. Someone took a

Polaroid picture of this event, and it stayed on my dad's refrigerator until the day we sold his house. Unfortunately, as his grief and alcoholism consumed him, he spent less and less time going to church. I know he appreciated the phone calls and visits from the pastors and his cousin, he rarely shared his grief. He kept all of his pain inside.

A year before my dad died I had a rare visit with him. He was completely sober, and we talked about his relationship with my mom, my childhood and his life. We looked through all the old photos from his childhood, and pictures from when he was still married to my mom. He opened up to me during this conversation, confessed things he did during his marriage to my mom and took responsibility for his choices and actions.

He had married my mom because she was pregnant with me, he said, but he declared that he was in love with her and really did want their marriage to work. He said that in the end, things were just too hard; too many things had gone wrong between them; too many accusations; too many arguments. In his mind and heart, it was too late and he let go of any hope he once had.

What I Know Now

Alcoholism is a reprehensible disease. It robs people of life and relationships.

My dad's desire not to confront or deal with heart issues runs deep within his family.

I regret not talking to my dad about the molestation accusation towards my ex-husband. We buried it deeply under the rug after he called me and I took Lauren to meet him for the first time.

Covering, ignoring or burying problems before you deal with them does not make them go away. They continue to fester under the surface.

106

I recognize I had an unhealthy fear of grief and I believe my dad had a similar fear. Grief is an emotion and I have learned that while it is not pleasant, I don't have to be afraid of it.

Strands of Hope

1. Have you ever struggled with an addiction? If so, what have you done towards breaking the cycle of addiction in your life?

2. Fear is usually at the root of not wanting to confront situations (fear of rejection, truth, emotions or abuse). Read Isaiah 43:2-3, Proverbs 3:25-26 and Psalm 18:28-30.

3. As you reflect on your personal relationship with Christ, is it a simple belief, or a lifestyle?

4. Read Psalm 119:2, Proverbs 8:17, Jeremiah 29:13 and Colossians 3:1-2.

5. Grief allows us to feel a distinct level of emotion at different times in our life. Read Isaiah 53:4, Matthew 26:36-39 and John 16:16-22.

CHAPTER 20

CONTROLLED BY FEAR

And you will know the truth, and the truth will make you free.

John 8:32

While Doug and I enjoyed our new life in Nashville, I continued to send Lauren's dad copies of her school papers, report cards and information on field trips, to give him a sense of being involved in her day to day life. Visitations were now limited to holidays, Christmas break and Summer vacation, but these visits diminished as the years passed. He made a lot of promises, but following through was a hit-or-miss proposition.

Shortly after we moved to Tennessee Lauren's dad re-married. Unfortunately, Lauren was witness to several violent situations between him and his new bride. I imagine plenty more went on that she wasn't aware of. That marriage ended in divorce within a few short years.

Although he lived thousands of miles away, my fear of him remained. I still would not confront him on any issues. I continued to allow things to be swept under the rug. One time Lauren came home from a visit and she mentioned how her dad had been a Japanese foreign exchange student in high school. She said they had gone out to dinner with his second wife and her parents to a Japanese restaurant, and her dad began telling stories of his experience in Japan as an exchange student. Lauren didn't recall ever hearing those stories before, but the way her dad spoke about this she assumed he had simply never mentioned this before. She believed his stories.

I know he was never a foreign exchange student. We went to the same high school and in our nine years together I never saw photos or memorabilia, or heard stories about it. I knew he was lying. He had always told outrageous stories, and most people never questioned him about them, even if they had a hard time believing what he said. I wasn't sure how to respond. I told Lauren that to my knowledge he was never a foreign exchange student either before or after we got married. Part of me wanted to call him and ask him why he told such an obvious lie. The more rational part of me knew better.

I chose not to confront him for two reasons; I didn't want him to get mad at Lauren for telling me and I did not want to feel his wrath. I figured he would find some way turn his actions around and make her the *bad guy*. I also knew how angry he gets when confronted with truth, and even though we lived thousands of miles away, I continued to stay within my self-constructed boundaries. I never confronted him.

Over time the skipped visits, missing promised presents, failed trips and lack of financial support became such an issue that I had no choice. I had to confront him. At those times the abusive man I knew so well came out - angry and cursing.

He told Lauren to never be afraid to ask for things that she needed or wanted. At times he came through on his promises. More often than not Lauren heard incredible stories of how her gifts were stolen or lost in the mail, or how due to someone else, he was unable to take her for the promised visit or trip.

He made a habit out of waiting for me to remind him of the monthly child support check. I dreaded the monthly reminder calls, but I played his game because I didn't feel I had a choice. It was stressful to month after month make that *friendly* reminder call when the agreed upon deadline for payment had passed. I found myself counting down the days until Lauren's graduation, all the while thinking, *Once Lauren graduates then I will not have to deal with him anymore. I can just say what I want to say.* But even as I thought it, I knew I was lying to myself. Who was I really kidding? I could never stand up to that man.

What I Know Now

I felt trapped in my relationship with my ex-husband, even though we had been divorced for several years, I was still functioning as an abused woman in our relationship.

Telling lies and outrageous stories, and manipulating people and situations for your own benefit, speaks to a deeper heart issue, usually involving low self-esteem, shame, fear and emotional issues.

Confronting someone is never easy, however God has given us an example of how to successfully and lovingly confront others in Matthew 18:15-17. This scripture refers to confronting other believers within the church, but I believe you can apply this concept to any confrontation.

Living in fear of anyone is not God's plan or purpose for relationships.

Strands of Hope

1. Do you know someone who has lied or exaggerated? Why do you think he or she did this? Do you think they were aware that you knew the truth? How did you handle the situation?

2. Confronting someone when you know that person is not being upfront or honest about a situation is never easy. After reading Colossians 3:9 and Philippians 4:8 how would you handle such a

110

confrontation?

3. Have you ever lied or exaggerated? How did you resolve this with God? How did you resolve this with the person you lied to?

4. Are there situations in your life today where you need to set up better boundaries, or seek forgiveness for overstepping your boundaries with someone else?

5. Are there times when you have agreed to do something, knowing you won't be able to fulfill the need, but you don't want to say no? Read James 5:12. How can you begin to change your approach to such requests?

CHAPTER 21

STRETCHING AND GROWING

Your word is a lamp to my feet, and a light to my path.
Psalm 119:105

Within two years of living in Tennessee, my relationship with my mom began to change. It had been several years since she had involved me in one of her episodes, but her drinking was starting to escalate, and once again the old patterns emerged. It was a Wednesday night and the kids and I were at church. Doug stayed home to try to get to bed early. Mom called our home phone and told Doug that she and my stepdad were arguing and she needed someone to come and get her. Doug did what he thought he should do - he picked her up and brought her to our home.

As I pulled into the driveway, Doug came out to greet us. "Your mom is inside," he told me, "and she's drunk."

My stomach knotted up, but I put on a brave face, and we went inside. Doug took care of the kids while I sat down on the couch with my mom. She cried. She told me she was afraid. I tried to remain calm as I sat there listening to the same things I had heard so often before. I was confused. She never spoke of being afraid when she was sober. What was I missing? What was really going on?

"I have a question I want to ask you," she said between sobs. "I want you to answer truthfully. It's okay, no matter how you answer. You won't hurt my feelings."

"Sure, Mom," I replied. "I'll tell you the truth. Ask whatever you want."

"Did you and your stepdad ever...*do* anything?" she finally managed to ask.

I was caught off guard, completely shocked by her question. I couldn't even comprehend the depths of her question.

"What do you mean, did we ever *do* anything?" I responded.

"I mean, did he ever touch you, or do anything sexual with you?" she said.

I was overwhelmed by her question. As I sat there processing her question I felt nauseous. My heart began to pound. Thoughts raced through my mind. *How long had she been suspicious of him? And if she did suspect her husband of molesting me, why didn't she say something sooner? And why didn't she try to protect me? Did she think we had an "affair"? Did something actually happen and I blocked something from my memory?*

Even as these questions played leapfrog in my mind, I answered her truthfully. "To the best of my recollection, my stepdad has never touched me or made any form of sexual advance towards me."

She grew calm and matter-of-fact, and said, "Okay." She asked for a glass of wine or a beer. I told her we didn't have any and I wasn't going to buy any. I asked her if I could pray with her, and she agreed, but as soon as I said "Amen," she said she wanted to go home. Doug drove her back to their apartment.

The next day I received the expected phone call saying she was sorry and that there would be – once again - no more alcohol in the house. Something stirred inside me as I listened to my mom, and before I realized what I was saying, I told her that she needed professional help and that next time she called me after she had been drinking, I would call the police to help her. I hung up the phone shaking and surprised by my outburst. No one had ever told my mom she had a drinking problem. And it was a big first step for me - it was the first time I had placed a boundary within my relationship with her.

As they usually did after a drinking event, things became relatively quite with my mom and stepdad. The next time we saw them, we all acted as if that last incident never took place, which was fine with me. I didn't want to continue the conversation, or thoughts that conversation had engendered. I had other things on my mind.

Doug and I had a major decision to make - whether we were going to stay where we were living or if we were going to move. We began praying about buying a house. One thing led to another and before we knew it we found a house in Franklin, Tennessee.

As paper work was being prepared for the purchase of our first home the unthinkable happened. Doug was let go from his job. The radio station he worked at wanted to change direction with their morning show and through no fault of his own, he was fired. This is an unfortunate down side to my husband's career - consultants can come on board and change the entire focus and objective of a radio station and before you know it, you've been told, "that was your last show."

To make matters worse, the man who fired my husband lived four houses down from the house we were purchasing. It was not an easy situation for any of us. We were friends. He was placed in the awkward situation that required him to make changes. I struggled with my anger toward him. I knew living in the same neighborhood and having to pass his home every day was going to be a challenge for me.

Then, as only God can do, within months of moving into

our new home, an opportunity opened up for reconciliation and restoration of the relationship. During an afternoon walk in the neighborhood with my daughter, we passed the man who had fired my husband. He was walking in the opposite direction so there was no opportunity to avoid each other. He smiled and said hello. I responded with a smile, said hello, and walked on past.

Then all of the sudden I found myself turning back and calling his name. He turned around and I took a few steps towards him. I felt uncomfortable, but I said, "I need to ask your forgiveness. I have been angry at you for firing Doug." He said he understood, and that he knew his wife would have felt the same way had he been in Doug's situation. He was sorry he had to make that decision.

I found myself wanting to go into detail, explain myself, and justify my feelings for the unfair way I felt my husband was treated. But God tugged on my heart - *Just apologize and don't justify it.* I told him while I appreciated what he said, I knew that I was wrong for holding onto my anger. He looked at me and said, "Okay, Sheryl. I forgive you." We smiled at each other and I thanked him. We turned and went our separate ways.

I felt such a relief as we walked away. This was the second time I was able to express myself in a healthy way; first with my mom, confronting her drinking problem and setting a boundary, and now this time, confronting someone that I was angry at, being free to say as much and also to ask for forgiveness. I was able to speak up and say what I felt in a way that was honoring to God, the person I was speaking to and to myself.

The loss of Doug's job was a time for our family to stretch and grow in our faith. While we were open to the idea of moving, if a new job were to require such a move, we were thankful that God allowed us to stay in our new home and within three months, Doug was offered a job at another local Christian radio station.

What I Know Now

Setting boundaries isn't intended to control others. Boundaries are guidelines for you to know what is acceptable and what is not in your own life.

Until an alcoholic desires to get help, the only thing you can do is decide what your personal boundaries will be with that person.

I was finally in a place in my life where I no longer wanted to sweep things under the rug.

The conversation and boundary I placed with my mom was a huge turning point in my relationship with her.

Asking forgiveness is humbling and there is freedom in forgiveness.

Strands of Hope

1. Prayerfully consider an area in your life where you need to place a boundary. Write down this boundary along with a realistic plan on how you can begin the process of living within the boundary.

2. Is there a person in your life that you have difficulty confronting with truth? While you can't be responsible for their choices or decisions, you can commit to pray for them daily and allow yourself to get to the root of why you are afraid to speak truth to them.

3. Think of a time when you asked someone to forgive you. What was their response?

4. Think of a time when someone asked for your forgiveness? What was your response?

5. Forgiving ourselves is often harder than forgiving others. Is there an area in your life that you need to forgive yourself? Read 1 John 1:9, Psalm 103:12 and Ephesians 1:7.

CHAPTER 22

GIVE HIM THE KEYS

As for God, His way is blameless; The word of the Lord is tested; He is a shield to all who take refuge in Him.

2 Samuel 22:31

Even as God was stretching and growing me in many areas of my personal life, I was still struggling with the issues related to my mom. I decided to make a counseling appointment with the women's ministry director at our church. I felt that I had scattered puzzle pieces of my life and while some pieces fit perfectly in place, other pieces appeared to belong to an entirely different puzzle.

I longed for things to be different in my relationship with my mom. I wanted what I believed other women had with their mothers; a close knit relationship. While my mom was close geographically, I didn't feel close to her emotionally.

It seemed to me that my mom was able to maintain a stable exterior façade, but emotionally and privately she wasn't. The alcohol turned her into a different person. When she was sober she got along well with my stepdad and others. Life appeared good and secure. She maintained her job and their home was always orderly and neat. She was friendly and had a sense of humor. She was dependable.

When she was under the influence the opposite was true. She was suspicious and angry. She would allude to horrible things my stepdad was supposedly putting her through, though never providing any specific details. She brought up situations and people who hurt her or offended her in the past -my father, her first marriage, family members, even old friendships she had let go of. If we appeared unsympathetic, disagreed or expressed a different opinion, she turned her tirade on us, reminding us of everything we had ever done (or not done) to hurt her. There was a price to pay for disagreeing, and none of us wanted to pay it. In the end, we usually just agreed with her or tried to change the subject.

With her instability, it was impossible for her to be the kind of mom I longed for; and quite possibly the mom she wanted to be. I never knew when she would start drinking again. I was always on guard. I found myself saying and doing things in hope of receiving her approval, and proving my loyalty towards her. It was another pattern I was comfortable with - a pattern I had been in since childhood.

My counseling sessions opened my eyes to a life changing concept; I needed to "give the keys" to my husband. I am a visual learner, so it didn't take long for me to visualize myself intentionally handing my husband a set of keys. The idea behind this phrase reminded me that my husband is my covering. God designed the husband as the head of the household, and one of his duties is to protect the family.

This whole time *I* had been in charge when it came to disruptions from my mom. *I* was also the one dealing with my ex-husband. *I* held the keys to these relationships. *I* was not allowing my husband to protect me or take care of me in those areas. Whenever something came up with my mom or my ex-husband I always talked to Doug about it, but I never considered asking him to step in or handle the situation. I was afraid to allow him to confront either of them, because I was unsure how he might deal with it. Even though I had grown spiritually and emotionally, I still had fear and anxiety issues, particularly when it came to confrontations with these two people in my life. I felt the need for their approval. I took drastic measures not to anger either of them.

My counseling sessions helped me realize I was afraid that if I allowed my husband to step in he wouldn't know how to "play the game" that I was unknowingly playing with them.

I talked to Doug about this concept and asked him to forgive me for not allowing him to cover me in this area. We talked about what this should look like in our marriage. We both needed to be aware of this behavior and agree on how and when he needed "the keys." I realized it was a trust issue on my end. I needed to trust him to have my best interest at heart. I needed to trust that he was seeking God's response in each situation. It was important for me to see how he handled situations. The more I gave him the keys, the less pressure I felt. This allowed me to slow down, take a look around and see things more clearly. As I did, certain pieces of my life's puzzle began falling into place.

It didn't happen overnight. It was a process. But as time has gone by, it has become a more of a natural instinct. It's made us a stronger team. Giving my husband the keys, emotionally and spiritually, involves trust and it is vastly different than being co-dependent. While I have struggled with co-dependency in the past, this process allows for teamwork and spiritual growth. We work together, and more importantly I trust that Doug has my best interest at heart. He knows that ultimately he is responsible for the way he leads us.

What I Know Now

The relationship I had with my mom was only a surface relationship. There were walls that I didn't realize were there before.

It was easier to give Doug the keys with situations regarding my mom than it was with situations with my ex-husband. The reason had to do with the level of fear and my PTSD.

God created men to be protectors and providers. By allowing my husband to help make decisions and support boundaries that we agreed upon, I was able to come under his covering and allow him to fulfill one of his God-ordained roles as husband.

Strands of Hope

1. Addictive behavior affects more than the addict, whether it's alcohol, drugs, pornography, gambling or any other addictive behavior. Is there an addiction in your life that you need to deal with?

2. One of the roots of co-dependency is seeing others as more valuable than you view yourself. Read Jeremiah 1:5, Romans 8:35-39 and Colossians 1:13-14.

3. If you are married, have you given the keys to your spouse? Why or why not?

4. Is there a relationship in your life that you wish was deeper than it currently is? If so, what is at least one realistic thing you can do to make positive changes in that relationship?

5. Encourage someone this week with an unexpected note, card or phone call...just because.

CHAPTER 23

THE MOVE THAT
OPENED THE DOOR

Seek the Lord and His strength; Seek His face continually. Remember His wonderful deeds which He has done. His marvels and the judgments from His mouth.

1 Chronicles 16:11-12

While I was finding comfort in the new "give him the keys" concept, God was further helping me by putting some physical distance between us and my mom and stepdad. After following us from California to Nashville, they decide to move to another state. This decision was sudden and unexpected. They informed us of their plans, and within a matter of weeks they were gone.

Several months later I received a drunk and emotional phone call from my mom saying my stepdad had left her. This was quite shocking to me. He had never left her before and to my knowledge had never threatened to leave her during the entire course of their thirty-plus years of marriage. She was the one who left, yet always returned a few hours later.

She asked if my sister and I would fly out and be with her. She would pay for the airfare. Within hours we each had a round trip ticket and were headed to be with our mom. Although she remained sober while my sister and I were with her, it was a stressful visit. I was grateful my sister was there with me. With a seven-year age difference, we had different memories and experiences growing up with my mom. Now as adults, united to help our mom, this visit ended up being a good opportunity for us to reconnect.

Together we tried to put the pieces together. We both wanted to finally know the truth about things our mother alluded to during her drunken rants. Was my stepdad really a mean, controlling person? Did he cheat on her? Did he abuse her?

When pressed for examples of my stepfather's unacceptable behavior, Mom offered two. Regarding his controlling nature, she said he was in charge of the TV remote and she never got to watch any shows she wanted. If she took something out for dinner that he didn't want, she had to put it back and eat whatever it was he wanted.

She insisted he was a brazen womanizer, that he flirted openly with bank tellers, grocery clerks and waitresses. She said he fondled these women's breasts in public. We were shocked.

"Why would all these women allow him to do such a thing in public?" we asked.

"Because they all liked it," she replied.

This conversation raised multiple red flags in my mind. I had known my stepdad since I was six years old. In all those years I had never heard or witnessed him act inappropriately or even flirtatiously towards any woman. If he was the controlling womanizer that my mom claimed, he did an amazing job of concealing it from me. When our visit was over I left feeling sad for mom, but happy that I connected with my younger sister. I was completely bemused about my mom and stepdad's life together.

I got a phone call from my stepdad, letting me know he had returned to Tennessee. He sounded hesitant on the phone. He wasn't sure where he stood with me. He struggled with guilt and shame about not being able to control the situation. He and my mom were masters of sweeping things under the rug and not dealing directly with them. They were also really good at not letting others in on their private life. It apparently all came to a head during their last intense argument.

A few months later, my mom decided she wanted to move back to Tennessee, although neither she nor my stepdad were interested in a reconciliation. To this day they are still separated. My mom was scared and lonely. She hadn't been on her own since her first marriage at age fifteen, and she did not like being alone. Without someone to help her maintain stability she became paranoid. She was convinced that she was being followed, that her phone was tapped and that people were *out to get her*.

I began to recognize patterns in my mom and stepdad's lives. They frequently moved from city to city, state to state or just apartment to apartment - always because someone did something that hurt or offended them. Mom left jobs because of someone else's behavior or some perceived slight.

I wondered whether other people really were at fault, or if it was just my mom's feelings and perceptions? Was my stepdad really a manipulative controller? Or were the patterns I was beginning to recognize all a combination of of both of their personalities? Neither of them had consistent or long term friendships. The one person I knew my mom to be friends with when I was in high school apparently offended my mom. Mom dropped the relationship without confronting the woman on the reason why.

It was as if they were always searching for a better place or a better situation. They tended to look for the negative in a person or situation, and usually found it. They appeared to expect to be hurt and were just waiting for that moment when they would be taken advantage of. From my perspective, they always seemed guarded and suspicious of each other and other people.

What I Know Now

The relationship my mom and stepdad had was quite complicated and I may never fully understand it.

I have never stopped loving, caring or praying for my mom or my stepdad.

I pray that my mom and stepdad seek God with their hearts, souls and minds. Psalm 9:10 - *"And those who know thy name will put their trust in thee; for Thou, O Lord, hast not forsaken those who seek thee."*

Strands of Hope

1. What are some red flags that you saw in past relationships that you ignored?

2. Have you ignored red flags in the past and later confronted them? If so, what was the outcome?

3. How does your family handle unhealthy behavior within the family?

4. Read 1 John 1:9 Focus on the truth of this scripture; it doesn't say only *certain* sins are forgiven. It says *sins* - period - and that God *is* faithful and righteous to forgive.

5. Are you currently sweeping anything under the rug in order not to deal with the situation? If so, what are two things you can do to begin the process of acknowledging and restoration?

CHAPTER 24

MORE...

*I would have despaired unless I had believed that I would
see the goodness of the Lord in the land of the living.
Wait for the Lord; Be strong and let your heart take
courage; Yes, wait for the Lord.*

Psalm 27:13-14

Once my mom moved back to Nashville, she quickly
morphed into someone I didn't recognize. She
began to use words and phrases I had never heard
her say before. She lost a lot of weight and started wearing
tight jeans and low cut tops. She changed her hair style. She
started making friends with young adults in their 20's. And
she began to drink...a lot.

The drunken phone calls didn't stop, but there were no more
apologies and no more promises not to have any more
alcohol in the house. She began dating a much younger man
who was an alcoholic and, I suspect, a drug addict. The
young man didn't have a job, didn't have a driver's license
and lived with his mother - a woman who, according to my
mom, hated her. Mom told me of their relationship and how
they had to sneak around. She made it sound as if they were
two teenagers who were in love but their parents would not
allow it.

Mom made connections with two young men from her
work. According to her, they wanted to use their friendship
with her to lure her into prostitution in a well-known red-
light district in Nashville. She was convinced her boyfriend
was in on their plan, and decided to trick him into

confessing. She thought the best way to accomplish this would be to get him drunk. She succeeded in getting him drunk enough to pass out. She was afraid he might have overdosed, and in a panic she called 911. It was hours later at the hospital before the young man regained consciousness.

Mom told us that her tactics worked - that her boyfriend had confessed his part in the plot on a message he left on her answering machine. I was anxious to hear the message to see if there was one shred of truth to back up my mom's outrageous story.

It should come as no surprise that the message on her answering machine did not contain anything remotely related to this alleged prostitution ring. All the message said was, "What happened? Where is my jacket? We got to talk, man. When can I see you? I don't know what happened. I need my jacket back. Call me back."

From that moment on, she became completely paranoid. She thought her apartment was bugged with video and audio surveillance. She lived in fear that the two young men from her work were videotaping her and waiting to force her into prostitution. At her request, Doug and I went to her apartment and looked over each and every hole in her stucco ceiling and walls. She wanted us to fill in any hole we could find with toothpaste.

There were no holes. There were no cameras, no recording devices. There was nothing, nothing at all. But facts have little effect on someone suffering from paranoia. My heart was breaking for the woman my mother was quickly becoming.

She was still convinced her boyfriend was in on the plan with the two young men from her work, so she broke off her relationship him and sought an order of protection from him. We accompanied her as she went to court to get a restraining order. As we are driving to the courthouse she told us there might be something on the police report about the night he passed out and she called 911 that might bother me.

"To get him to confess, I agreed to smoke crack with him," she said. "But I didn't really smoke it. I only pretended to smoke it."

I wasn't sure how to respond to this confession, but I didn't believe she *only pretended.*

As we entered the court room I felt my anxiety grow. I had no idea what other surprises might pop up. I was also curious to see the man my mother was involved with. I spied him sitting across the room. He was my age, but he appeared much older. He looked haggard and worn out.

His mother was also there - an older, neatly dressed woman with a permanent scowl etched across her face. It was obvious she did *not* like my mother.

The judge called my mom and her ex-boyfriend to the stand. Since no one argued or disagreed with the order, the judge stated the expectations, they both agreed and the order was put into effect. That was that.

All the drama that my mom was ensnared in compelled her to want to move again. It didn't take long for her to put plans in place and move. During the entire episode I allowed my husband to be my protector. He *had the keys* and whenever my mom called, he answered first. Often we let the call go to voice mail. If she sounded sober, I would call her back. If not, I ignored it. At times, she would get very drunk and make the round of phone calls: first to my stepdad, then to my sister and finally to me if she wasn't satisfied with their calls. I have no doubt she would then call other family members or friends until they eventually put a stop to it as well.

She once called when I was sound asleep and I accidentally answered the phone. It didn't take long to realize she was drunk.

"I'm sorry, Mom," I told her. "But I'm tired and I have to work in the morning, so I cannot continue this conversation now."

She became angry with me and hung up, but within seconds she called back. I woke Doug up and he told her that we were sleeping and if she needed emergency help she should call the police. She responded with, "Oh, sorry to bother you" and hung up.

My boundaries were up and it did not take my mom long to realize that in order to speak to me she had to go through my husband. As a result, the calls came less frequently. When she did call and leave a sober message, I called her back; with Doug right there, ready to take the phone if she started sounding drunk or angry. This is still our practice to this day.

The beginning of placing boundaries within my relationship with my mom, the counseling I was receiving and the writing I have done, has put a deep divide between my mom and me. She had cut all communication with me for several years and only recently have we started the slow process of communication again.

The boundaries I have in place weren't easy to establish, especially within my heart, but they have helped reduce my level of anxiety and given me the space I needed to begin the healing and restoration process. There are times I find myself wishing everything would go back to the way it was, but I know that is not healthy. My mom has to deal with her addictions and emotional issues before either one of us could ever consider what a mother-daughter relationship would look like for us. I love my mom and I haven't given up hope for her. I know that God is in control but I cannot give her the help that she needs. I can't save her. She needs to make those choices for herself.

What I Know Now

No matter how Doug and I felt about my mom's situation, I knew it was real to her, which is why we continued to try to help her as best we could with our boundary in place.

In order for me to accept the relationship that I had with my mom, I had to grieve the loss of the relationship I desired.

No amount of indulgent behavior will change your situation or ease your pain, it will more than likely ruin relationships and create more problems for you.

Although my mom has not been diagnosed, to my knowledge, I am sure she experienced an emotional breakdown after the separation with my stepdad, which contributed to her paranoia and odd behavior.

There is always hope. Isaiah 43:25 - *"I, even I, am the one who wipes out your transgressions for My own sake. And I will not remember your sins."*

Strands of Hope

1. Is there a person in your life that you desire a deeper or closer connection with, but it's impossible due to circumstances? Write the person's name down and commit to regularly pray for him or her and the situation.

2. Have you witnessed someone you care about go through a complete physical, emotional or spiritual transformation? Was it positive or negative? How did this impact you personally?

3. Have you had to grieve the loss of what you wanted or expected in a particular family member relationship?

4. Describe what you think and feel it means to grieve over a relationship.

5. Read Psalm 31:9, Psalm 147:3, 2 Thessalonians 2:16-17 and John 14:27.

CHAPTER 25

LAUREN

*These are the things which you should do: speak the truth
to one another; judge with truth and judgment for peace
in your gates. Also let none of you devise evil in your
heart against another, and do not love perjury; for all
these are what I hate, declares the Lord.*

Zechariah 8:16-17

My daughter Lauren was a senior in high school and preparing to graduate May 2006. As spring arrived and plans for her graduation ceremony and party were underway, I was an emotional mess. Not only was I stepping into a new season of life with my daughter, I was worried about having her dad being here along with my sister, whom he was accused of molesting. Lauren knew nothing of the accusations. I had been able to keep a boundary between my family and my daughter's father...until now. The upcoming celebration of her high school graduation had the potential to blur that line.

Lauren's impending graduation date opened the door for me to have a much needed and long overdue conversation with my sister, Shelli. It was a hard conversation. I was uncovering a subject we had carefully tucked under the rug many years before.

I asked Shelli to forgive me for not protecting her. She forgave me. She said she had forgiven me years ago.

We talked about everything - from the first time he touched her inappropriately, to the day she and my dad told me about

132

the incidents. There were many tears shed during this conversation. I regret allowing this situation to be pushed under the rug for so long. By not talking about it with anyone, except my husband, I allowed it to hold me captive. I was now beginning to understand the power of forgiving myself.

I sent Lauren's dad an email, letting him know that my sister and family would be there. I carefully avoided saying anything that could be taken as an accusation or innuendo. I was preparing to send him another email, telling him that he needed to plan to see Lauren before or after the graduation party. The idea of having him at our house along with my family was too much for me to handle. I wanted my family, especially my sister Shelli, to be a part of this special day in a safe, comfortable environment. If my ex-husband was there, I knew it would be incredibly uncomfortable for everyone involved.

I didn't have to send the second email. Once he learned that my sister and family would be present, he informed me that he wasn't sure he was coming. He had already began to pull away from Lauren, and I was afraid not showing up for her graduation would surely put more distance between them. I wanted to confront him about it, but I confess it was an emotional struggle. I knew Lauren wanted her dad to be a part of this milestone in her life. On the other hand, if he didn't come, I wouldn't have to worry about any potential confrontation between him and my sister.

Unfortunately, I still hadn't completely given my husband the keys in this relationship. I was still holding onto the anxiety and stress of trying to be in control. Since Doug didn't have the keys, he was unable to completely cover me spiritually like God created him to.

Within a few days of our email exchange my ex-husband

called and said he wanted to explain why he had been pulling away from Lauren. He said he was sick; that he had been diagnosed with Parkinson's disease. I pressed for details, but he remained vague. He was an artful storyteller and had the ability to weave a small amount of truth into a lie. He was convincing and I never knew what to believe. Even though I doubted his story, a small part of me wondered if he was telling the truth.

I told him I was sorry he was dealing with this, and that I hoped things would get better for him.

He sent Lauren a text message saying he would not be able to attend her graduation due to his health issues. The night before her graduation he sent her a simple text saying, "Congratulations." This hurt Lauren deeply. While I was tremendously relieved that he wasn't coming, I felt the pain Lauren was experiencing at not having her dad genuinely acknowledge her biggest accomplishment at that point in her life.

After that congratulatory text to Lauren all contact and financial support came to an abrupt halt. Phone calls were not returned, emails not responded to, text messages ignored, certified letters sent to him were returned. It was as if he dropped off the face of the earth. None of his relatives or friends knew where he was or what he was doing.

I was sad for Lauren, but selfishly I was also relieved. After all of the years of anxiety, fear and walking on egg shells I was finally in a position where I wouldn't have to communicate with him anymore.

Following graduation was an intense time of helping Lauren prepare for the transition of college. I felt it was also an appropriate time for her to seek counseling, especially in light of her father's disappearance and how it was affecting her. It was also time for me to talk opening with her about everything - my marriage to her father, my sister's accusation - and answer any questions she may have. I also wanted to ask her about her relationship with her dad. I felt it would be better for both of us if we had a counselor walk with us through the depth of the details.

Much she already knew or pieced together on her own over the years. The hardest thing to talk to her about was the situation with Shelli. She had no idea. She wasn't sure what to think or feel. Out of all of my siblings, Shelli was the one Lauren was closest to. I honestly don't know how someone in my family didn't make a comment or say something about the situation to Lauren over the years. I guess it shows the power of sweeping unpleasant situations under the rug. But Lauren was becoming an adult. She was going off to college. I did not want her to hear this from anyone else - she needed to hear it from me.

What I Know Now

I am grateful that my sister and I finally "lifted the rug" and talked about the accusation.

I know I am forgiven by God and my sister, but I will always regret my response to the accusation and situation.

Emotionally preparing for your child to graduate high school and move on in life is not easy, and every parent deals with their emotions differently.

Giving my husband the keys has made our relationship stronger.

Strands of Hope

1. Is there something from your past that you need to confront, acknowledge or confess?

2. Read 1 John 1:9 and James 5:16.

3. Confronting difficult situations is not easy. Write

down a practical plan along with biblical references on how to confront a challenging situation or person.

4. Have you ever been disappointed by someone that didn't acknowledge or celebrate an accomplishment or goal in your life? How did you respond, and why do you think this affected you the way that it did?

5. Putting our disappointments and feelings aside is not a natural response, but we can acknowledge our feelings without allowing them to control our response or behaviors. Read Philippians 4:6-8.

CHAPTER 26

FAITH AND LETTING GO

*The name of the Lord is a strong tower; The righteous
runs into it and is safe.*

Proverbs 18:10

The summer of 2006 was an emotional season - talking
to Lauren about my relationship to her father, the
molestation accusation, her father's disappearance,
the preparations (emotionally and physically) for her to start
college - it was a lot to take in. She planned on attending a
college that was less than 90 minutes away, but the idea of
her being away from home for an extended amount of time,
was hard on me.

The day came when we packed all of her things and headed
out to drop off her at college. Bad news hit as soon as we
arrived on campus. The college dorm she was assigned to
was abruptly shut down due to a recently discovered mold
problem. Hours passed before a meeting was called between
the college president, the students and parents. Two choices
were offered. The students could either stay at a hotel within
walking distance to campus until a dorm room could be
secured, or they could elect to stay at a nicer hotel that was a
10 - 15 minute drive from campus.

I was disappointed and anxious. This wasn't how I
envisioned my baby girl starting her first month in college.
We spoke with the college president and determined that the
hotel that was in walking distance to the school was the best
option. Being closer to campus seemed like the more logical
and safer option, and the president assured us that the

campus police were available if needed, as an added measure of security.

The first several months were a struggle. I tried to put on the *brave mom* face, especially when I was around others. But at night when everyone was asleep, I would go to her room, lay on her bed and cry tears only a mother can understand. I prayed that God would protect and guide her.

Within days of starting college, Lauren met a young man and jumped into a serious relationship with him. This relationship came out of nowhere and moved fast. Throughout her high school years, Lauren's friendships were mostly in group settings. She went on a few dates, but she never pursued a serious dating relationship. During her senior year of high school she read the book, *I Kissed Dating Goodbye*, and made a firm decision that the next person she dated would be her husband.

I couldn't put my finger on it, but I felt uneasy about this young man and his rush to become serious with my daughter. Lauren said several things that raised red flags to my mind. I couldn't understand why she didn't see them. I wanted to respect and trust her choices, and I didn't want to push her away. I fought for balance between faith, trust, letting go and my mother's instinct. Doug and I prayed diligently for this young man, and I specifically asked God to help me see and love him, like He does, instead of how I felt.

The first time I spent time with Lauren's new boyfriend, I recognized similar traits that Lauren's dad had; not the anger or violence, but the need to have a *big story*. His stories always seemed outrageous or painted him to be the victim. Like Lauren's father, nothing bad that happened was ever his fault. He claimed to be a Christian, but I didn't see any fruit in his life. He wasn't interested in doing Bible studies or devotions because, he said, he had already read the Bible. He claimed to know the Bible, but could never articulate anything about his faith.

Doug and I brought up these red flags to Lauren, but she was determined to make it work. She tried her best to make him look good to us. We invited him over for dinner several times and he tagged along on various family outings. Each time I prayed that God would help me see him through His eyes and not my own.

I never felt a peace about him. I was anxious and afraid for Lauren. I didn't think he would physically abuse her, but I knew this was not the man I had spent Lauren's entire life praying for.

What I Know Now

Never stop praying for your children, never stop asking questions and never give up.

1 Peter 5:7 says, *cast all your anxiety upon Him because He cares for you.*

Finding the balance of parenting a college-age young adult is often complicated and at times heartbreaking, but if it's done with the right intentions, prayer and love, it is possible.

I am glad I shared my concerns with my daughter openly instead of sweeping my feelings under the rug.

Speaking truth in love involves uncomfortable conversations.

Strands of Hope

1. Have you been in a situation where others around you saw things you didn't see or that you chose to ignore?

2. Have you confronted someone with what you perceived as red flags with regards to their choices or

relationships? What was their response?

3. How do you manage the balance of trying to control a situation to obtain a desired outcome, and trusting God's will and timing?

4. Read John 14:27, Psalm 27:14 and Proverbs 3:5-6.

5. Have you made a choice that you now regret? Are you are now concerned with someone you care about making that same decision? What are some things that you can do to share your concerns with this person?

CHAPTER 27

PANIC AND FEAR

*When you pass through the waters, I will be with you;
And through the rivers, they will not overflow you. When
you walk through the fire, you will not be scorched, Nor
will the flame burn you.*

Isaiah 43:2

December, 2006. Lauren was home for Christmas break. I was relieved to have her back at home for an extended amount of time without her boyfriend around. It was close to midnight. Doug, Garic and I were asleep. Lauren was in the front room watching TV.

I was startled awake when Lauren came running into our bedroom. "Mom," she cried out. "Get up! Someone is banging on the front door and screaming your name!

I stumble out of bed, not fully conscious and forgetting that Doug was sleeping next to me. I banged into the china cabinet as I ran to the front door, resulting in a huge, painful bruise that graced my thigh for weeks. A woman's cry pierce my groggy consciousness as I approached the front door.

"Sheryl, help me! Sheryl help me," the voice repeated over and over.

I peered through the peephole, but could see no one. The voice sounded like my mom, but that conclusion made no sense. She had moved out of the state. If the person banging on my door was she, when did she come back to Tennessee? Maybe it wasn't my mom, but whoever it was, she obviously knew me. I was scared. I was starting to panic. But I knew

141

one thing for sure - I was not going to open the door until I could see who it was.

Suddenly the banging shifted to my son's bedroom window, which faces the front porch. I ran to look out that window, but couldn't see anyone. The person continued calling out my name, but this time she was back at the front door. I ran back to the front door, but by the time I got there, she was back at the window. I was terrified!

I grabbed the phone and dialed 9-1-1. Doug was now awake and coming toward me out of the bedroom. For some reason I had not even considered waking him up.

"9-1-1; what's your emergency," the voice on the other end of the phone asked. I explained what was going on while trying to get a glimpse of the woman through the peephole. Then I saw her. "I think it's my neighbor," I told the operator, "but I am not sure."

Our neighbor had moved into the house a little over a year before. It was common knowledge in the neighborhood that she worked in the adult entertainment industry and that she was involved with pornographic websites. She had previously told me she was involved in business development and traveled often. She even joked with me that people sometimes assumed she was in a particular line of business, simply because she had enhanced certain body parts.

I had made the decision to be friendly towards her despite her chosen profession, but I never broached the subject. I didn't want to make her uncomfortable. The only reason I could fathom that God allowed her to move into our neighborhood, and right next door to us, was for me to reach out and minister to her. I brought her food when she was sick, I picked her up from the hospital when she needed a ride home, I made a point to talk to her when I saw her outside, even if it was a simple, "Hello."

She never acknowledged her *real* job and I let her believe that I didn't have a clue. But I did know the truth, and there were several other red flags that caused me to mistrust her. I kept a firm boundary in my relationship with her.

I thought the 9-1-1 operator told me to open the door and tell her the police are on the way. I snapped! I threw the phone to Doug, put my back firmly against the door and said, "I can't open the door." I started crying, while Doug tried to tell me that I didn't need to open the door.

"All you need to do is tell her that help is on the way," he said.

I looked through the peephole once more and saw her standing on the porch. "The police are on the way," I called through the door.

"Okay," she whispered, then walked back to her house.

We watched through the window as moments later several police cars arrived. We only opened the front door when we saw an officer standing near our side of the lawn. There was a pair of stiletto heels near our porch steps. I took them to the officer.

"I think these belong to my neighbor," I said. "Would you make sure she gets them back?"

"Can you tell us what's going on," Doug asked him.

The officer said, the woman said she had been attacked and robbed by a couple that she had invited into her home. That was all he could tell us for now.

The next day we saw her outside. I asked if she was okay. She said she was sorry and apologized for scaring us. I also apologized for not opening the door, but that I wasn't sure who it was. I was afraid and trying to protect my family.

"They drove off after the attack," she explained. "My purse

was in their car, and my cell phone was in my purse. I don't have a land line. That's why I came to your house. I wanted to call the police."

Something changed inside me that night. I couldn't explain, nor did I understand it. I continually questioned why God, allowed this woman to move next door to us? I was uncomfortable pretending that I didn't know who she was and what she did. I didn't trust her before, and this incident did nothing to change my opinion. I tried to make sense of it all, but it didn't appear to make any sense at all.

What I Know Now

I was trying to find the balance of loving the sinner but hating the sin. I didn't want to judge her because of her choices. After all, who among us is without sin?

As I struggled with letting her know I knew the truth about her, this placed me back into old familiar patterns that I was no longer comfortable with, but I didn't know what to do about it.

Once my husband was awake and involved, I was afraid that he might open the door assuming she was safe because she wasn't a "stranger." Because of my distrust of her, I feared if he did open the door our family would be in danger.

Strands of Hope

1. Have you experienced knowing the truth about a person or situation only to *feel* that you must pretend that you don't? How did you respond to this?

2. What advice would you offer to someone who is struggling with sweeping specific knowledge under the rug, in order to give the illusion that they don't know the truth?

3. Read John 4:1-30 for a clear example of Jesus

speaking truth in love and loving the sinner but hating the sin, with the Samaritan woman at the well.

4. Find another clear example in the Bible of someone confronting someone else with truth, even if it appeared uncomfortable.

5. Not every situation requires us to confront someone who is choosing to live in denial or confess the truth to us. Consider how you would know when to speak up and when to simply allow God to deal with the situation.

CHAPTER 28

STORM CLOUDS GATHER

The LORD is my shepherd, I shall not want. He makes me lie down in green pastures; He leads me beside quiet waters. He restores my soul; He guides me in the paths of righteousness For His name's sake. Even though I walk through the valley of the shadow of death, I fear no evil, for You are with me; Your rod and Your staff, they comfort me. You prepare a table before me in the presence of my enemies; You have anointed my head with oil; My cup overflows. Surely goodness and loving-kindness will follow me all the days of my life, And I will dwell in the house of the LORD forever.

Psalm 23

My life, as I knew it, was getting ready to take a huge turn. I had no idea how the incident involving my neighbor combined with the emotional freedom I felt from not having to communicate on any level with my ex-husband, would kick start the process of allowing my brain to work through and unpack a lifetime of situations and events.

It had been eight months since my last contact with Lauren's dad. I found out from other family and friends that he systematically cut off contact with everyone. Lauren was apparently the last one. I also discovered that he had been in a drug and alcohol recovery program several years earlier that I knew nothing about. I suspected that his lack of contact with Lauren had more to do with a possible current drug and alcohol problem, rather than any diagnosis of Parkinson's disease.

146

Only in hindsight can I see God's hand all over this. It was His perfect timing for my *storm* to hit, and the ultimate healing it would engender, both emotionally and spiritually. It needed a spark to start the process. My neighbor's situation was the spark. It uncovered the memories I had so conveniently pushed under the rug. I never forgot them, I just ignored them, and now they came crashing back with a vengeance. I had no choice but to face them.

My neighbor, pounding on my door and screaming for help in the middle of the night, unearthed the memory of the night I sought help from a neighbor, so many years before. I had always told myself if a woman ever came knocking on my door for help, no matter the situation, I would help her - just like my neighbors helped me. I struggled with guilt for not opening the door. I've since come to realize that I did help her. I called the police. And that was the best thing I could have possibly have done for her.

Seeing and feeling the huge bruise on my thigh from bumping into the china cabinet - something I had never done before or since that night - reminded me of my bruises from past abuse.

The odd relationship with my neighbor, knowing her secrets but pretending I did not, camouflaged acts of service and compassion for her were all examples of me falling back into my old habits. I knew there was balance between compassion and honesty, but it was more convenient to go out of my way to make her feel comfortable, even when I was extremely uncomfortable with the situation.

I now know why God allowed her to be my neighbor: He allowed her to be a trigger. The reminder of past abuse, not having any contact from my ex-husband for eight months and allowing myself to fall back into unhealthy, non-confrontational patterns, worked together to allow my brain

147

to begin to process what I had been suppressing for so long. Subconsciously I knew I was in a safe place and I needed to confront my past.

In the midst of all of this, Lauren's relationship with her boyfriend was progressing at a rapid clip. Doug and I genuinely tried to accept the young man. We wanted to see the good in him. I prayed for him daily, but each time I prayed *for* him, it was as if God showed me more and more reasons to pray *against* him. My heart was torn for my daughter. I could see clearly this relationship was not healthy, and certainly not God's best for her. I was concerned for her and knew enough that I didn't want to ignore the red flags that I saw.

One particular incident made it abundantly clear that this young man did not care about our family and had repeatedly lied to us, and we knew it was time to set a firm boundary. We had already caught him in several lies. We felt that he had put Lauren in dangerous situations on more than one occasion. He created a pattern of keeping her all to himself. We began to notice she was letting go of friends and activities that she loved. Her grades suffered as every minute of her time was consumed with this young man. After months of praying we were prepared to tell Lauren that we would no longer support this relationship. While she would always be welcome in our home - he was not.

I knew it was the right thing to do. I also knew it had the potential to push her deeper into his arms. I had to decide if my love for her was strong enough to sustain our relationship, if she chose him over our family.

I had never implemented such a strong boundary with anyone before. I knew it had the potential to break my heart. But Doug and I were in agreement. It was something we had to do to protect Lauren and our family.

Three days, before we had planned to talk with her, I was in the Emergency Room feeling as if I was dying.

What I Know Now

God's timing is not always our timing, but it's the best timing.

Ecclesiastes 3:1 *"There is an appointed time for everything. And there is a time for every event under heaven."*

Tough love is hard.

Red flags usually never change color.

I felt powerless to change my daughter's mind about her boyfriend. The reality is that I was. It had to be her choice. I had to continue to pray that God would open her eyes and heart to the truth.

Strands of Hope

1. Is there a time in your life that you can look back and see God's plan and purpose, but at the time you found yourself questioning God?

2. Write down all the ways that you can now clearly see how God had a plan and purpose for your situation.

3. Establishing and following through on boundaries can be challenging. Write down three scriptures that can encourage you when you are faced with such a challenge.

4. Have you ever prayed for a loved one to open their eyes and heart to God's truth, as well as the veracity of the situation they are in? What was the outcome, or are you still praying?

5. Read Proverbs 27:12. Consider all of the ways you can begin to apply this verse to your everyday life.

CHAPTER 29

THE STORM HITS

For I am convinced that neither death, nor life, nor angels, nor principalities, nor things present, nor things to come, nor powers, nor height, nor depth, nor any other created thing, will be able to separate us from the love of God, which is in Christ Jesus our Lord.

Romans 8:38-39

January 27, 2007 - 12:30 a.m. I woke up from a deep sleep feeling nauseous. I thought I must be coming down with the flu. I attempted to sit up and get out of bed, but I grew more nauseous. I wondered if I would make it to the bathroom, which was only a few feet away. Without warning a hot flash raged from my neck to my groin. My heart rate accelerated. I couldn't catch my breath and began gasping for air. I laid back down and I tried to calm myself by taking small, slow breathes. The nausea subsided a bit and I felt a moment of relief.

A huge wave of nausea washed over me accompanied by an even more intense hot flash. My heart felt as if it was trying to pound its way out of my chest. It hurt, and I was scared! I was trying to remain calm and breathe, but there simply wasn't enough oxygen in the room to fill my lungs.

I touched Doug and whispered to him, "I think I am very sick." He woke up instantly, but as he sat up the nausea and chest pounding intensified exponentially. I thought I was dying.

"Call 9-1-1," I whispered.

Within minutes both an ambulance and the fire department arrived. They settled me on the gurney while asking Doug for as many details about my condition as he could give them. All I could think about was that I wouldn't be able to say goodbye to my kids. Lauren was away at college and Garic was still asleep. As they loaded me into the ambulance, Doug promised to get Garic and meet us at the hospital.

On the drive to the hospital Doug tried to remain calm for Garic's sake. They prayed that God would heal me from whatever was going on. I had several more attacks on the way to the hospital. I did not want to die in the ambulance. I pleaded with my eyes to the paramedics, *please don't let me die!*

I was given an IV and medication that was supposed to calm my heart rate down, but even with the medicine my heart rate only dropped to 140 beats per minute. A normal heart beats in the range 70-100.

God let me live, I silently pled with God. *I will be a better Christian and example for my family and friends. I want to grow old. I want to someday have grandchildren. Please God let me be okay!*

Doug and Garic arrived shortly after the ambulance. I asked Doug to call Lauren and tell her I love her, although I wasn't sure if Doug could get through to her. She was in her dorm at college and most likely sleeping. She was accustomed to turning her cell phone off at night, so there was no way to make sure she knew what was going on until she woke in the morning.

I felt there were things I needed to tell my husband - things I wanted him to know, in case I really was dying. Garic reached out to touch me.

"It's okay Mom," he said. You're going to be okay. God will protect you."

"I know, son," I put on my brave face. "I need you to know

how much I love you and how special you are to me. Never forget that okay?"

He leaned across the hospital bed, gently kissed me and told me he loved me too. Doug took a hold of Garic's hand and placed a hand across my body and began to pray. They prayed that God would heal me and give the doctors wisdom and discernment as to how to help me.

Several hours later and after many tests, EKGs, X-rays and a treadmill stress test, the only thing they could find wrong was low potassium. The attending physician prescribed anxiety medication and a potassium supplement, and sent me home with instructions to follow up with my family doctor.

My family doctor saw me briefly before I was discharged. She thought I had experienced a panic attack. I wasn't familiar with the term. *Panic attack* sounded to me like another term for *worry wart,* and while I certainly worried about things, I knew this could not be anything as *simple* as a panic attack. There was something wrong with me! Every test came back negative and I was feeling better. But I knew one of two things happened: either they missed something or God chose to heal me of whatever had invaded my body so violently.

What I Know Now

Panic attacks are real.

Panic attacks can make you feel like you are dying.

How long we live and whether we have physical or mental health problems is not a reflection of how good we have been or could be. We will never be good enough. That is why we have grace and why Jesus willingly sacrificed himself on the cross.

No one deserves what Christ did for us. We can not earn salvation or God's grace. It is a gift from God. God longs for a relationship with us. We don't have to bargain to get it.

Strands of Hope

1. Have you ever experienced a panic attack? If so, what are some things that you were able to do to get through it?

2. Has there been a time when you tried to bargain with God to answer a prayer that you were desperate for? Read 2 Kings 20. If you were in King Hezekiah's place would you have chosen to live the last 15 years as he did? If not, what do you think you would have done differently?

3. If you knew you had a certain number of years, days or even minutes before you breathed your last, whom would you want to spend time with? Is there anything you feel you need to communicate to anyone before you die?

4. Worrying about things, whether they are in our control or not, is an area of struggle for many people. Make a list of the things that you find yourself worrying about. Separate the list into two columns. One column for worries that you can control and the other for worries over which you have no control (i.e. someone else's behavior, choice or response, disasters, weather, unexpected events or challenges, illness or death).

5. Read Psalm 55:22, 2 Timothy 1:7, Psalm 112:7, Philippians 4:6-7 and Deuteronomy 31:6. Write these verses down and post them in places that remind you to let go of what you cannot control, and that you can make strong and courageous choices on what you can control.

CHAPTER 30

LET THE HEALING BEGIN

Heal me, O Lord, and I will be healed; Save me and I will be saved, For You are my praise.

Jeremiah 17:14

Once we were home from the hospital I followed up with my family doctor and she gave me an anti-depressant, which I reluctantly took. She was insistent that I'd experienced a panic attack. I did not feel *depressed* and I did not understand why she wanted me to take an anti-depressant. I still didn't believe I had a panic attack. I wasn't even sure I believed there was such a thing as a panic attack.

Within the span of a few weeks I became a believer. I had several more serious panic attacks which resulted in three Emergency Room visits, another ambulance ride to the hospital, a multitude of tests and several other doctor visits. The whole time we prayed for God's healing touch, and for wisdom and discernment for the doctors who were treating me. We called our church and asked for prayer. Many family members and friends prayed diligently for me. One of our pastors and an elder in our congregation came to our home and prayed over me and anointed me with oil in accordance with Scripture. Doug talked about my situation during his radio show, and thousands of people I have never met prayed for me and sent notes of encouragement.

During my third Emergency Room visit, one of the nurses listened compassionately as Doug and I began to relay all of the details over the previous months. She agreed with my family doctor that my symptoms sounded like a panic or anxiety attack.

"I have a family member who had similar symptoms," she said. "They saw a doctor who worked with them and now they are able to manage those attacks. The important thing to realize is that these attacks are real. They are not something you are just making up, and can make you feel as if you are dying."

As we left the Emergency Room and headed home with new medications and directions to follow up with my family doctor, I began to wonder if maybe I really was experiencing panic attacks. And I wondered, if I was having panic attacks, why was I suddenly having them now? And what can be done about them?

I went to work researching panic and anxiety attacks, then I connected with a local psychiatrist. It was important to me to find a doctor who was familiar with panic and anxiety attacks, and she was. She helped me understand that the brain is a powerful tool; that it protects us and at times shields us from dealing with issues that are traumatic, stressful or emotional. At some point in time, either when you feel safe or when you have been triggered in such a way, your brain will allow you to uncover what needs to be dealt with. That is what happened to me.

As I look back over my life, I can see early signs of panic and anxiety in me. I also know the moment my brain felt safe enough to release all that pent-up anxiety - when my ex-husband seemed to disappear from our lives, and my mom had moved away, and I had started placing boundaries in that relationship. My neighbor's situation was the trigger.

Not everyone who has experienced trauma earlier in life will have a severe panic attack like I did. It might be smaller. It might come out in a different way; emotional instability, depression or it could even manifest as a physical illness.

In my naivety I asked my doctor how long she thought I might need to be on medication and in therapy. I was hoping she would say, "Maybe a few weeks." She could not give me an answer...or a time line.

"Every person is different," she explained. "Everyone responds to medication and therapy in different ways. Part of the answer to that question depends on you."

I decided immediately that I would pursue my recovery with a passion. I wanted to be better. I wanted to move forward. I wanted to pull every scrap of my history out from under the rug and deal with it. I realized it would be hard and emotionally draining, but I was ready to face it all - all of the guilt, shame and fear that had been my constant companions since early childhood.

I felt God allowed this door to open, even though it wasn't something I would have chosen on my own. I was grateful and relieved to have someone walk with me through this treatment and offer hope. My husband faithfully and steadily encouraged and supported me throughout the entire process. Shortly after confirming my diagnosis of panic and anxiety, she also diagnosed me with PTSD (Post Traumatic Stress Disorder), and prescribe a different anti-depressant along with a panic and anxiety medication to help when I had the attacks.

Several months into therapy my doctor felt the next level of treatment was EMDR (Eye Movement Desensitization and Reprocessing). It sounded a little too New Age for me, and I wasn't interested in having anything to do with New Age philosophy or hypnosis. But I trusted my doctor and she assured me that she was familiar with the positive results EMDR can achieve. I researched EMDR on my own and discovered that it has been successfully used for over 20 years and proven helpful for people who have had trauma in their life. It has nothing to do with either New Age philosophy or hypnosis. My doctor was confident that I would benefit from this therapy and after prayerfully talking with my husband, we agreed this was the next step for me.

I started seeing an EMDR therapist in September 2007. EMDR reprocesses traumatic or stressful memories. It doesn't erase them, but it does help you to process them differently so that you will not be triggered with panic, anxiety or fears.

Through this therapy I have been able to go back into my memories and have compassion for who I was. I am not a victim; I am a survivor. I now have an understanding of why I made certain decisions at specific times, or didn't speak up at other times. I've gained insight into some of the choices I made. I am also more aware of co-dependent patterns and unhealthy relationships.

Along with my therapist I created a basket of tools to help when I am facing an anxious or stressful moment, such as:

Breathing - Deep breathes in and out.

Removing myself from the situation, even if it's around the corner for just a moment. Close my eyes and breathe.

Peppermint! My symptoms always start in my stomach with nausea.

Ginger tea - I keep ginger tea bags on hand at all times. I breathe in the smell of the tea and slowly sip it, feeling the sensation of the warm tea going down my throat trying to focus on this sensation rather than my anxiety.

Slowing down and listening to the sounds around me.

Keeping hydrated - I always keep a water bottle near me.

Taking a few moments, when needed, to sit down in a quite

room and close my eyes (a few minutes can make a huge difference).

Being aware of triggers. Some things bother me more than others. I have to be aware of how my mind and body are reacting to it.

Prayer and reading the Bible. I write scriptures on index cards and post them on mirrors or cupboards.

Physical touch. A hug or hand squeeze, comforting textures like a soft blanket, a fluffy pillow can help reduce stress.

Keeping a journal. Writing things down has been helpful; thoughts, feelings, memories, prayers, etc.

Listening to soft instrumental music.

Communication. Always talking things over. I now work hard at not letting things fester or get pushed under the rug.

Acknowledging the choices I have. Maybe I can't change the situation, but I can choose how I handle it, if I stay in it and what I want to do about it

Medication.

I have learned there is no quick fix when you are dealing with issues of the past. It takes time and commitment. It is important to focus on one day at a time, which is challenging for me, because I want to rush to the finish line; I want to be done.

It is also important to find the right doctor and treatment plan that works for you. I was fortunate to connect with my doctors at the beginning. I know others who were not as fortunate. I encourage anyone who is looking for a doctor or counselor to make sure there is a connection. It's important that they specialize in the area you are struggling with.

I also believe in taking medication if your doctor feels it will help you and it is not abused. There is no shame in taking an anti-depressant or anxiety medication. Taking medication does not mean your faith is lacking or you're not right with God. If you had high blood pressure or diabetes you wouldn't think twice about treating your illness. Depression, anxiety and panic attacks are no different. Because we live in a fallen world we are exposed and predisposed to any number of physical or mental illnesses. I believe God can choose to heal you miraculously, but each person and situation is unique. It's not up to us to put God in a box and say how He will choose to heal, or when He will heal.

Once you begin to pull things out from under the rug and see things from different perspectives and understanding, you will begin to recognize more of who you are. I am aware, more than ever before, of my struggles with boundaries, co-dependency, lack of confidence, low self-esteem, forgiveness issues (accepting forgiveness, forgiving others and forgiving myself), fear of grief, taking responsibility for other people's choices and ignoring red flags. I am learning to have compassion and understanding towards myself - not excusing my choices or behavior, but digging deeper to understand why and slowly change what I can.

What I Know Now

The tools in my basket work well for me and I have to remind myself at times to use them.

As I've learned more about myself, my trigger, and how my body responds, there have been times when I have tried all of my tools and ended up taking medication to ease the panic attack, and that's okay.

I will always have panic and anxiety, but as my husband reminded me, "It will never be like it was in the beginning."

You can never unlearn what you have learned.

159

I believe God can use doctors and medication, or He can choose to heal miraculously. Either way is appropriate and Biblical.

I must choose daily to allow my faith to be bigger than my fears.

Strands of Hope

1. What are some tools that you can use the next time you feel anxious, fearful, ashamed, tempted or angry?

2. Write down specific quotes or scriptures from this book that can encourage you when you need it the most.

3. Read Isaiah 12:2. How can you apply this verse to your life?

4. Has God opened a door that you would not have chosen to open on your own? What was the outcome?

5. What are some areas of growth that you are willing to be intentional about in your life?

CHAPTER 31

THE POWER OF FORGIVENESS

*The end of a matter is better than its beginning; Patience
of spirit is better than haughtiness of spirit.*

Ecclesiastes 7:8

After a year of ceaseless prayer, concern and letting my faith become bigger than my fears, Lauren broke up with the boyfriend in August of 2007. Unfortunately, this decision plunged her deeper into a prodigal journey. Doug and I were blinded from seeing the full extent until the end of her sophomore year at collage. She was ready to confess and repent. She wanted to return home, get a job and pursue a few classes online for the next year. She has a powerful testimony that she shares and we have plans to minister together in the near future from a mother-daughter perspective.

Once Lauren began to pick up the broken pieces of the previous two years, she wanted to find her father and forgive him. I struggled with this the moment she told me she felt God was leading her to call her dad. I wanted her to have peace in her heart and to follow through on what she felt was God's leading, but I was concerned his response might hurt her. And to be perfectly honest, I was anxious about how it might affect me.

It only took one phone call to find him. She left him a message reaching out with love and forgiveness. He responded promptly and soon they were moving forward with renewed hope in their father-daughter relationship. I was able to maintain a balance of being there for her without getting involved. This was their relationship - there was no need for me to be drawn into it.

Almost a year after Lauren returned home from college, she met the young man that I knew beyond a shadow of a doubt was the man I had been praying for from the time she was born. Several months into their dating relationship, Stephen proposed and Lauren accepted!

The news of Lauren's engagement ushered in waves of excitement. With the renewed relationship between Lauren and her father, she wanted all three of us - her father, Doug and me - to walk her down the aisle. My initial reaction was to jump back into fear mode. I began to second guess every potential scenario that could find us face-to-face.

I was well aware of the growing anxiety within me and knew that I needed help working through my thoughts, feelings and possible confrontations. My emotions were on high alert. I had made amazing progress, but now I felt like I was beginning to back pedal. I wanted to be *done* processing memories about my ex-husband.

I realized I was giving him too much power and control over me, but I didn't know why or how to stop. As my doctor continued to work with me, I recognized that even though I thought I had forgiven him, under the deep roots of our past was a lingering sense of unforgiveness. I was afraid to completely forgive and move forward. If I did, I felt he would no longer be responsible for those actions.

I equated forgiveness with reconciliation, and the thought of reconciling with him drove me to an emotional place that I hadn't been to in quite a while. I was *angry* at him. I didn't *want* him at the wedding.

I was also concerned that my dad's side of the family, specifically my sister, Shelli, wouldn't come if he was there. There was a part of me that didn't want to deal with all of that - and there was another part of me that knew God had a plan and a purpose, and that through this situation I would continue to grow stronger.

Through prayer and my therapist, along with continued EMDR, I was able to work through every feeling. I began to understand forgiveness on a much deeper level. Forgiveness does not take away or diminish the responsibility of the offender. The ultimate responsibility rests solely between the offender and God. Forgiveness frees me to move forward. Forgiveness doesn't mean you must reconcile with the offender - sometimes distance or a firm boundary is necessary for everyone involved. Reconciliation can be as simple as putting an end to a conflict. By completely forgiving my ex-husband I let God handle his consequences, and I allowed my heart and mind to put a final *period* in our story.

My therapist encouraged me to think like a queen. Queens are confident, dignified and respectful. If my ex-husband made a comment or said something that I was uncomfortable with at the wedding, I could calmly look him in the eyes and say, *"This is Lauren and Stephen's day and I choose not to respond at this time,"* then confidently and respectfully turn around and walk away.

I was concerned with being forced into a fake friendship with him. I didn't want to pretend we were friends, like he told others we had been years ago. I didn't want to feel obligated to hug him or shake his hand. I began to understand it was okay to say, *"No thank you,"* if a hand is extended.

I was shocked at how easy that could be. It may seem obvious to many people, but for me it was a life-changing concept. I had been a people pleaser and co-dependent most of my life. It never occurred to me that I had the ability to say, *"No, thank you."* It doesn't have to be rude or in an angry tone. It is possible to say it confidently, in a dignified and respectful way.

My daughter's wedding was a memory I will treasure forever. She was a beautiful bride - and yes, all three of us walked her down the aisle. She and I started the walk together. Half way down the L shaped aisle, Doug met us and linked arms with me. Almost at the end of the aisle, Lauren's father linked her other arm, and the three us presented her to Stephen.

I made sure to completely give the keys to Doug that day, and he faithfully accepted them. He handled all communication that needed to be shared and was a shining example to me of being a man of honor and integrity. The day went off without a hitch.

My sister, Shelli, and the rest of my dad's side of the family came, as well as other family and friends. The ceremony was lovely and the reception was enjoyable. At the end of the day Lauren's father came towards Doug and me and extended a hand towards Doug. Doug shook his hand. He then turned towards me and said, "Congratulations." I took a small step back. I stopped, took a deep breath, straightened my back, looked him in the eyes and replied, "Thank you. And you as well." He and his girlfriend smiled and walked away. I continued to enjoy the remainder of the evening with my daughter, my new son-in-law, and my family.

What I Know Now

I am grateful that my daughter was repentant and had the faith and courage to confess and accept consequences and boundaries. She faithfully moved forward and I am proud of who she has become.

My initial feelings about Lauren contacting her dad were not unexpected, given our history. While I did not wish him any ill will, I needed to establish a boundary. I had to work through what that needed to look like and feel like in order for me to feel safe and confident.

As hard and uncomfortable as it was seeing Lauren's dad, I am glad I had the ability to work through everything and move forward in a spiritually and emotionally healthy way.

It's okay to decline a hand shake or excuse yourself from a conversation if you're uncomfortable.

Forgiving someone does not negate what they have done. Forgiveness releases you from carrying their burden and allows it to be between them and God.

Forgiving someone does not mean you have to go back to unhealthy relationship patterns. You can forgive and still maintain firm boundaries.

Strands of Hope

1. Have you experienced a prodigal in your family? If so, who and where do things stand now?

2. Read 1 John 1:9, Proverbs 28:13 and Acts 3:19.

3. Is there someone in your past who spoke truth into you and at the time you disregarded their words? If so, prayerfully consider sending them a note letting them know their words or actions may have seemed to fall on deaf ears, but they did take root.

4. Think of a time when you uncomfortably acknowledged or continued a conversation with someone you felt uneasy around. Would you do anything differently now? If so, what?

5. Is there something holding you back from forgiving someone? If so, what is it? Are you ready to move forward?

CHAPTER 32

LOST AND FOUND

*Now may the Lord of peace Himself continually grant
you peace in every circumstance, the Lord be with you all.*

2 Thessalonians 3:16

L OST

There was someone noticeably missing at Lauren's
wedding, and that was my mom. By the time of the
wedding she had stopped all communication with
me. My mom knew about my panic attacks and that I had
been diagnosed with PTSD. I shared bits and pieces of my
therapy with her, and she was aware that writing had become
an important tool in understanding and moving forward for
me.

When I shared with her that God was leading me to turn my
writing into a book to minister to others, she was surprised,
but she never asked direct questions. I shared certain details
about the book, but I remained intentionally vague.

Part of the process of working through things was allowing
myself to grieve (again) over the reality that the relationship
I wanted with my mom did not exist. I expected that the
little that remained between us would most likely disappear
once she read the book. I had to ask myself if there was any
hope for the future by exposing the past and all the things I
worked so hard to keep under the rug.

The day came when she asked how the book was coming
along. I told her it was about to be released, and she asked
me to send her a copy. My heart sank. I told her I would.

It was only a few months before Lauren's wedding. After much prayer, many tears and working through a plethora of thoughts, feelings and reactions with my doctor, I mailed a copy of book to her. I included a letter explaining that it was important to me that she knew I was willing to talk about anything related to the book. But I also wanted her to know that I had specific boundaries in place if we were to talk about the book. I reminded her that the book is about me; it was about my memories, my feelings, how I recalled things. I was not judging her. I was not blaming her or anyone else. I ended the letter by telling her I loved her and that I prayed she will seek the help she needs emotionally and with her alcoholism.

Almost two years after I mailed the book I received a letter in the mail from her. It was short and to the point. She asked that I no longer send pictures or gifts to her.

I cried. I grieved over her request. I saw the communications I had been sending to her as safe because I kept things centered on my children and my life in a generic form. It was my way of staying attached in an inconspicuous way. To cut off all communication seemed to cut the frayed and tattered cord that loosely connect us.

I respected her request, yet there was a deep sadness in my heart for the loss of a mother-daughter relationship.

FOUND

Before the communication I had with my mom was over, I was able to be the catalyst in reuniting her and my older brother, LeRoy. After thirty years of wondering what happened to him, and if he was even still alive, I received news from an unexpected source. I connected with someone on a high school memorial page, and asked if he or anyone he knew might be able to help me find my brother. Within hours I received information on how to contact him. I was shocked - all of the years I tried to locate him and within hours someone else came up with information and good news!

It was important to me that I communicated to my brother that I wanted this to be about me and him. I didn't want my mom to know I had been looking for him, nor that I found him. I also didn't want to get stuck in the middle if I told her and she rejected him. He agreed and was beyond happy to connect with me after all these years. After several months of catching up with each other, he asked me if I would consider giving our mom his phone number and telling her he loved her. He made it clear he didn't want anything from her except to have her as a part of his life. He assured me he wasn't angry or mad, and wanted the past to be the past.

After talking to Doug and praying about giving my mom my brother's message, I felt a strong urge to do it. Deep down I think I knew that my time of communicating with her was drawing to a close.

I was calm and matter of fact when I shared the news with her. Her initial reaction was skeptical. I assured her of his intent and encouraged her to reach out to him, and several days later she did. That was the beginning of the renewal of their relationship. I am grateful that my brother has been able to connect with her and they have been able to move forward in a way that is good for both of them. When I think about the timing, and how God used me at just the right time to connect my mom and brother, it brings me an extraordinary sense of peace.

FOUND

Two years from the time that my mom requested that I no longer communicate with her, my brother was the catalyst in connecting my mom and me again!

Through a series of unexpected and life changing

circumstances regarding her finances she found herself in dire need of help. My brother knew that I would be concerned and took this opportunity to ask her if she would be willing to talk to me. She said, *Yes*.

During our initial conversations she told me she had been sober for a few years. I could tell from our conversation that she was indeed sober. It's been a slow process for us. We still have boundaries in place; we stay on "safe" subjects. I am taking things one conversation at a time. I know at any moment something can be said or misinterpreted, by either of us, that could end the communication that we have started. I have held onto hope and will continue to hold on to it. My heart's desire is to follow God's will and use every opportunity I am given to speak life and hope into my mom and her situation.

I am grateful God used my brother to play a significant role in my life; finding him, reuniting him with our mother, and his part in reconnecting me with my mom after several years of silence between us.

What I Know Now

Matthew 19:26 - *With God all things are possible.*

My mom set a boundary of her own with me by requesting no more communication, photos and gifts. As hard as it was to accept it, I did.

I know beyond a shadow of a doubt that I was supposed to write this book and encourage others.

In order for me to move forward, I needed to go back to my beginning to acknowledge and understand certain patterns, behaviors, choices and reactions.

There are times when, like Lot's wife (Genesis 19:1-26), I am tempted to look back and yearn for what was, even though it was unhealthy; it's what I knew.

I considered not telling my mom about the book, but I knew if I did that, it would be going back to patterns of putting it under the rug, and I have worked too hard to revert back to doing that.

Strands of Hope

1. Have you prayed for reconciliation or restoration of a broken relationship? How can you see God working in this situation?

2. Read Matthew 19:26 and Romans 8:28. Write these down on and index card and place them where you will be continually reminded of God's promises.

3. Is there a time frame in your life where you were tempted to look back and yearn for what was? If so, how has that impacted you today?

4. Have you experienced reuniting with a loved one after years of being apart and not knowing what happened? What was the outcome?

5. Boundaries are often difficult to place in relationships. Boundaries only work if you are willing to enforce them. Is there a boundary that you need to consider placing? If so, prayerfully seek wisdom in deciding what that needs to look like and the best way for you to implement it.

CHAPTER 33

THE JOURNEY CONTINUES

Great is our Lord and abundant in strength; His understanding is infinite.

Psalm 147:5

I consider myself always to be *in process*. I continue learning things about myself and my relationship with God, and I strive towards having healthy relationships in my life. There are days when I feel strong and confident, and there are other days when I know I need to persevere, no matter what I am faced with.

The most significant lessons I have learned throughout all of this are:

1. Don't ignore red flags (and if you find yourself in a situation where you know you have, it's never too late to do something about them).

2. Don't take responsibility for other people's choices or behavior.

3. Don't allow yourself to sweep anything under the rug. Not everything needs to be confronted, but if you find yourself in a situation where it does, take courage and press forward.

4. In order to completely embrace all that forgiveness offers, you need to think of forgiveness as a triangle - forgive others, forgive yourself and accept Gods forgiveness. All three points are important.

5. Forgiveness does not erase what someone has done; it takes the control that the situation/person has over you away

and places it where it belongs - with God.

6. Boundaries are okay. Boundaries look different for each person and situation. Only you can decide if a boundary is needed in a relationship, and what that boundary should look like.

7. Know your triggers and have specific tools in your basket to help you cope when you are triggered.

8. Allowing yourself to dig to the root of unhealthy patterns, choices or relationships, past or present, takes courage and determination. It's not easy, but it is freeing. I encourage you to take the steps necessary towards wholeness and hope.

9. I am not alone and neither are you. There is no such thing as a perfect person and it's time to stop listening to the lies from the enemy. You matter. You are loved. God created you with a plan and a purpose.

10. I started off with a scarlet cord of guilt, shame and fear. Today, that same cord represents God's redeeming love, abundant grace and unending forgiveness.

There is always *Hope!*

ABOUT THE AUTHOR

Sheryl Griffin is first and foremost a wife and mom, but she is also an author, speaker and encourager. With extensive training and experience in early childhood education, Sheryl has been involved in children's, youth and women's ministry for more than two decades.

In 2007, Sheryl began suffering from debilitating panic attacks and was consequently diagnosed with Post Traumatic Stress Disorder. Her quest for answers to the many questions she had regarding her past led her to the realization that God had bigger plans for her than just answering those questions. He was calling her to share a message of hope, grace, mercy, forgiveness and freedom.

Sheryl tells her story at retreats, conferences, women's events and family programs. If you are interested in having Sheryl speak at an event please contact her at:
sheryl@sherylgriffin.com

You can keep up with Sheryl on her website and blog at:
www.sherylgriffin.com

ALSO AVAILABLE FROM
WORDCRAFTS PRESS

Donkey Tales
Exploring Perspectives of the Bible's Stubborn Creatures
by Keith Alexis

Chronicles of a Believer
by Don McCain

More Devotions From Everyday Things
by Tammy Chandler

An Unlikely Evangelist
by Paula K. Parker

Youth Ministry is Easy!
...And 9 other lies
by Aaron Shaver

WordCrafts